THE SEEKER'S GUIDE TO

Jesus in the Gospels

Other books in the Seeker Series include

Living the Beatitudes Today
Bill Dodds and Michael J. Dodds, O.P.

The Seeker's Guide to Being Catholic
Mitch Finley

The Seeker's Guide to Building a Christian Marriage
Kathleen Finley

The Seeker's Guide to Reading the Bible
Steve Mueller

The Seeker's Guide to Saints
Mitch Finley

The Seeker's Guide to 7 Life-Changing Virtues
Bill Dodds and Michael J. Dodds, O.P.

The Seeker's Guide to the Christian Story
Mitch Finley

The Seeker's Guide to the Rosary
Liz Kelly

Chicago

THE SEEKER'S GUIDE TO

Jesus in the Gospels

LOYOLAPRESS.

CHICAGO

STEVE MUELLER

LOYOLAPRESS.

3441 N. ASHLAND AVENUE
CHICAGO, ILLINOIS 60657
(800) 621-1008

The Seeker Series from Loyola Press provides trustworthy guides for your journey of faith. It is dedicated to the principle that asking questions is not only all right, but essential.

Portions of chapter 3 previously appeared as "Thoughts on the Thirtysomething Jesus," *The Bible Today,* March 1999.

Cover template and interior design by Lisa Buckley
Cover image: Betty Crowell/Faraway Places

Library of Congress Cataloging-in-Publication Data

Mueller, Steve.
    The seeker's guide to Jesus in the Gospels / Steve Mueller.
      p. cm.—(Seeker series)
    ISBN 0-8294-1551-3
    1. Jesus Christ—Person and offices—Biblical teaching. 2. Bible.
N.T. Gospels—Theology. 3. Catholic Church—Doctrines. I. Title. II.
Seeker series (Chicago, Ill.)
    BT203 .M84 2001
    232—dc21   2001038070

Printed in Canada
01 02 03 04 05 06 07 08 09 Webcom 9 8 7 6 5 4 3 2 1

Contents

A Word to the Seeker

If Jesus Christ were to come today
people would not even crucify him.
They would ask him to dinner,
and hear what he has to say,
and make fun of it.

—THOMAS CARLYLE (1795–1881)

Two centuries ago, Scottish essayist and moral teacher Thomas Carlyle prophesied what Jesus' fifteen minutes of fame might be like in our media culture. Yet despite our secular sophistication, which enjoys making fun of belief and things religious, we are still fascinated with Jesus.

His image is everywhere. He appears on the cover of *Time* magazine and as the subject of TV specials, movies, novels, and rock operas. Scholars form a Jesus Seminar to debate and vote on which words and deeds Jesus really said and did.

Big business uses Jesus' birth as an excuse for the biggest binge-buying months of the year. Consumers are glutted with Jesus items—T-shirts, statues, holy cards, and an infinite variety of cultural artifacts bearing his likeness or challenging people to consider WWJD (What Would Jesus Do?). As a Japanese student once remarked, "The strange thing about Jesus is that you can never get away from him."

To the Christian disciples of the first century the conception of Jesus as a rabbi was self-evident, to the Christians of the second century it was embarrassing, to the Christian disciples of the third century and beyond, it was obscure.

—JAROSLAV PELIKAN
theologian and Church historian, *Jesus through the Centuries*

The book business is also booming as studies about Jesus proliferate. As John the author of the fourth Gospel said at the end of his Jesus book almost two millennia ago, "There are also many other things that Jesus did; if every one of them were written down, I suppose that the world itself could not contain the books that would be written" (Jn 21:25).

I have tried to present briefly and clearly what is needed to understand Jesus today. The information in this book is not entirely new, for every Jesus book deals with the same familiar range of topics: his identity and titles, his teaching, parables, miracles, suffering, death, and resurrection. But the approach and arrangement of these topics is my own. These are my conclusions after almost forty years of seeking to answer Pilate's sardonic question to Jesus, "What is truth?" (Jn 18:38).

In every decade we instruct Christ as to what He was and is, instead of allowing ourselves to be instructed by Him.

—*AMOS N. WILDER*
theologian, *Theology and Modern Literature*

But this was not the only question Jesus was asked. Several other questions that sincere seekers put to him appear as the epigraphs for the chapters of this *Seeker's Guide.* Their seekers' questions can help us learn more about who Jesus was and what he was doing.

There are, of course, no limits to the questions we might like to ask Jesus. I hope that from answering the questions in this book you will discover the Jesus you search for.

I would also like to thank all the seekers over the years who have helped me sharpen the questions and polish the answers in my search for Jesus. I especially thank Bruce Smith for reading the manuscript and wearing out his red pen seeking more felicitous phrases.

My greatest debt of gratitude is to my wife, Mary, and to our four children—Margaret, Luke, Johanna, and Drew— who are the living icons of Jesus for me. In their eyes and their hearts, in their words and their deeds, I have daily discovered the presence of God once more incarnate.

Two veils keep us from seeing the living truth of Jesus. One veil is our ignorance. . . . The other veil is that we think we know, but in truth we are just accustomed to hearing the same words, episodes, statements over and over again.

—*ROMANO GUARDINI*
(1885–1968), German theologian, teacher, and popular writer, *The Lord*

A WORD TO THE SEEKER

PART ONE

Who Are You?

(John 8:25)

What are you looking for?

—*JOHN 1:38*

CHAPTER ONE

Seeking the Identity of Jesus

Near the beginning of the Gospel of John (1:35–40), there is a story of two would-be followers of Jesus. When they finally met Jesus, he asked them the question that confronts every seeker: "What are you looking for?"

As you begin your search for Jesus, you have to decide what you are looking for. What is it you really want? Like these first seekers, you may want to know Jesus because you have a hunch that he can teach you something. But what is it you want to learn?

Each of us will have his or her own emphasis, but certainly one thing we all seek is to live a genuinely human life. If we want to learn how to live as fully as possible, Jesus offers us an invitation to see the world and evaluate it as he does so that we can live in it with the same sense of commitment and courage, grace and beauty.

For almost two thousand years, people have been seeking to know about Jesus, just as they do Buddha or Muhammad or any other religious person, because these persons seem to teach us who God is and what human life is all about. Their words, their actions, and their whole style of life offer us something to imitate.

Thanks be to the Gospel, by means of which we also, who did not see Christ when He came into this world, seem to be with him when we read his deeds.

—*ST. AMBROSE*
(ca. 339–397), bishop of Milan, *Concerning Widows*

Jesus, a Jew from an obscure village in Roman Palestine, is certainly one of the most influential persons in human history. Christians believe that Jesus lived and died and rose to new life and that in him is the key to the relationship between all humanity and God. So for them he is not just a personality from out of the past but someone who is alive in a new way and continues to be present in the world and in Christian communities. His presence continues to be an effective influence over these communities and the way they carry on his ideas and mission.

Knowing Jesus remains possible today primarily through the writings in the New Testament of the Christian Bible.

Jesus continues to be available to us through his words and deeds, reported in the four versions of Jesus' life that are called Gospels. These reports, because they express the inner mystery of Jesus as a person, allow him to come alive for us when we read them. Reading Jesus' words in the Gospels invites us into a personal dialogue through which we can get to know him despite his absence in the flesh for over two millennia.

Discovering Personal Identity

Seeking to know another person is a complex and difficult task. We spend a lifetime trying to answer two haunting questions: Who am I? Who are you?

Individual identity is not a simple, global insight into another person but a complex construction of multiple identities gathered from experiencing that person in many different circumstances. Identity is not something we just know, but something we form over time by our participation in different relationships. To discover someone's identity we need to examine this intricate network of relationships.

In fact, we are different people in different situations. We live simultaneously in many different spheres—family, work, community, church—and each sphere is characterized by specific experiences, values, expectations, vocabulary, demands, and affiliations. Who we are can vary widely in our various social settings as well as in political and religious

spheres. Yet all these personas are united through five important factors—our name, our body, our voice, our situation,
and our story. These factors give us our sense of personal
identity.

Seeking Jesus' Identity

There is no one identity that summarizes everything about
Jesus. We must seek to know him in the same way we seek to
know others. We cannot be content with knowing his name.
We must also learn about his body, voice, situation, and story
in order to discover who he was and the meaning of what
he did.

Jesus' Name

Names and their derivations were often considered significant in biblical times. *Jesus,* a derivative of *Joshua* (Hebrew,
"Yahweh saves," *Yahweh* being the personal name of God),
was a common Jewish name. It recalled the famous ancestor
Joshua, the zealous assistant to Moses. When God prohibited
Moses from entering the Promised Land, Joshua took over
the burden of leadership. His brilliant military victories and
conscientious religious dedication enabled the people to
cross the Jordan into the Promised Land and create the conditions for a life according to God's directives.

So it is no wonder that, as people looked back on Jesus' life and ministry, they would make connections between his accomplishments and those of his namesake, Joshua. They would look for ways to understand how Jesus was indeed a leader like Joshua. As God's agent for saving people, Jesus would win the final victory over God's enemies and enable a new covenant people to cross over into the promised kingdom of God to create the community that God always desired.

Jesus' Body

What Jesus' disciples took for granted, we are denied. We have no photographs of Jesus, in fact no physical descriptions of him at all. He remains forever faceless except through the creative power of our individual imaginations.

Although we know nothing about his specific height, weight, facial features, or mannerisms, each of us sees him with our imagination when we form an image of what he looked like. We can be pretty certain, though, that the first-century Palestinian Jesus did not resemble our Hollywood image of a young, white, blue-eyed, brown-haired man with perfect teeth! There is no reason to think that he didn't look like most Jewish men of his day; there is no mention, even in the Gospels, of any unique, identifying features. There's never a guarantee that our personal image corresponds in any way to the real Jesus. We actually have a better indicator of Jesus' unique personality through his words.

Jesus' Voice

Jesus remains available to us through his words. Although we no longer experience the human voice of Jesus as his disciples once did, he continues to be recognized through his words, which were remembered and gathered by the community of his disciples in the Gospels. Despite academic arguments over which particular words Jesus might or might not have spoken, biblical scholars all recognize the consistency and uniqueness of the voice of Jesus presented in the four Christian Gospels.

Jesus' Situation

Jesus lived in a particular place and time: Galilee in the northern part of Roman-occupied Palestine in roughly the first thirty years of the first century (4 B.C. to A.D. 30). He was a first-century person at home in his own world. He understood his world and how to operate in the first-century political, social, and cultural spheres as a Jew living in Palestine.

Christ is not a person for me but a hero, a myth, an extraordinary shadow image in which humanity has painted itself on the wall of eternity.

—HERMAN HESSE
(1877–1962), German poet and novelist

Seeking the identity of Jesus requires that we discover him in this first-century situation. One of the greatest dangers is to unconsciously re-situate Jesus as a twenty-first-century person and assume that he understood the world as we do and was guided by concerns and interests similar to our own. His situation was not ours, and appreciating what his world was like is one of the most important challenges any seeker faces.

Jesus' Story

After Jesus' death, his story was certainly told and retold orally by the first Christians as they sought to learn from his life and teachings. About forty years after his death, as the Christian communities struggled with questions about their own identity in the face of persecution by the Romans and rejection by the Jews, four coherent narratives of Jesus' story, the Gospels, were composed by the writers we identify as Matthew, Mark, Luke, and John.

These recollections contain what Jesus' followers thought of him, and only indirectly what he thought of himself. Through their accounts of his words and deeds, we can reconstruct who he was and what he was striving to accomplish by using our imagination and what we know of his times.

Seeking Jesus' Identity through the Gospels

Everything we know about Jesus we know secondhand. He left no writings, no autobiography, no soul-searching diary of what his life was all about. We have only the reports of his followers, shared, collected, and shaped after his death, as the primary sources for discovering his identity. There are other sources we now know about, such as the comments of Roman and Jewish historians, but the Gospel accounts remain the primary sources.

The Gospel lives of Jesus were collected by the first-century Christian community and joined with certain other Christian letters and writings to express the authoritative meaning of the new Christian covenant (New Testament) with God. The New Testament books are the official collection of texts (the canon) chosen by the Christian church. These texts were chosen from many texts available, and there's much about the process of selection that we don't know. But it is clear that the Christian community believed that these writings expressed the essential truths about the community's relationship with God through Jesus and the Holy Spirit.

These writings also provide the most important resources for understanding Jesus' identity. In their various ways, all of the New Testament books were composed to help the early Christians discover who Jesus was and what it meant to be his disciple. By learning from these books who God was, who Jesus was, what God was doing through Jesus, what the Christians' relation to God was, and what their role in God's plan was supposed to be, Christians found a way to understand more fully their identity as Christians. They were the community that was called into being by God's word and the example of Jesus, and their purpose was to realize God's dream of people living in the right relationship with God and with one another.

These Gospel lives of Jesus formulated Jesus' identity in a way that was also meant to shape the identity of those who read them. The life story of Jesus was the pattern for the life story of every Christian. The Gospels were tools for the conversion of disciples into imitators of Jesus. Their strategy was to persuade readers to identify with Jesus and the disciples in the story, and follow Jesus as disciples did. These four Gospels were the first, and still most effective and indispensable, seeker's guides to Jesus.

For this reason, the Christian Gospels are the most reliable presentation of who Jesus was. They are the essential starting point for any inquiry into who Jesus was and what happened to him. We must recognize, of course, that this portrait is the "official" portrait shaped by his Christian disciples to present and defend their claims about Jesus the Christ as the model and primary example of who they were as Christians.

Knowing the First-Century Jesus

How would Jesus have answered the question of his identity for his followers or for his Jewish inquirers? What were the different faces he showed to people that revealed who he was?

Because every society has its own way of identifying people, in our search for Jesus we must first consider the kind of information first-century people would have wanted in order to know who he was.

In the culture of Jesus' place and time, the group, not the individual, came first. People understood their identity in relation to the groups to which they belonged. A shorthand way of understanding a person's identity was to know the three *Gs*—gender, geography, and genealogy.

Gender. In a society where everything depended on one's male or female status, a person functioned primarily in either the male realm (external, public, dominant—the marketplace) or female realm (internal, private, subordinate—the household). These realms established a whole set of expectations about each person's character, roles, status, abilities, and possibilities in life. Jesus lived in and dealt primarily with the male sphere of public interaction, competing with others for his share of honor, status, and recognition.

Geography. In a society in which many people seldom ventured more than thirty or forty miles from their village, one's identity became strongly linked to a sense of place. The ancients thought that the particular combination of elements and climate that made up the environment directly influenced the physical and mental characteristics of the persons who lived there. Jesus was from the obscure village of Nazareth, in the hilly mountains of Galilee in northern Palestine. We'll explore further what it meant at that time to be from Nazareth.

Genealogy. In first-century Palestine, family membership determined much about a person's identity and place in society. Because the family was structured according to patriarchal power and authority, the father was the hub of family relationships. Not only was it virtually impossible to have a family without a father, but within the family the father, as the only real adult, embodied the family's honor, represented the family to the outside world, and did all the thinking and talking for the family members. Jesus' family, the household of Joseph of Nazareth, was neither wealthy nor of high status. This we will look into in more detail in a later chapter.

Where Our Seeking Will Take Us

In chapter 2, we will look more closely at Jesus in his environment and consider the important first-century clues to his identity—gender, geography, and genealogy—and discover the man Jesus of Nazareth in Galilee.

In chapters 3 through 6, Jesus' important relationships provide us with a lens through which we can understand him. He was a "son" in several different ways: a son in his family, in his religious and ethnic heritage, in his new community, and in his relationship to God. Each of these "sonships" will help us understand who he was, what he did, and why he did it.

Each of these sonships also confers a title of honor on Jesus. These titles are clues to the public honor and status that Jesus claimed and that the Gospel writers wanted their audience to acknowledge. These "honor claims" also create expectations about the kind of behavior that such a person ought to exhibit.

In chapter 3, we consider Jesus as the son of Joseph and Mary. We will look at information from the Gospels about Jesus' family and examine two other clues found in the Gospels: his age and occupation. Jesus was a "thirty-something" carpenter when he left his family to begin his public ministry of announcing and building God's new kingdom community.

In chapter 4, we will explore his identity as Jesus the descendant of Abraham and David, the Jewish Messiah sent by God as the divine agent who would restore the broken relationship between God and God's people. The messiah, or anointed one (Greek, *christos*), was a particularly Jewish identifier; in order to understand what that title meant, we will look at how *messiah* shifted in meaning throughout Jewish history and what Jews of Jesus' time expected of their messiah.

In chapter 5, we examine Jesus as the bearer of the new age. In that role, Jesus spoke of himself as the "Son of man." Heavily indebted to Old Testament prophecy, this self-designation can mean simply a human being, or it can take on an association with the end times, when God will send a divine agent to inaugurate the final transformation of our world. This title, "Son of man," holds Jesus between the human realm and the divine realm, and thus thrusts him into a "more than ordinarily human" form of existence.

I tell the Hindus that their lives will be imperfect if they do not also study reverently the teaching of Jesus.

—*MAHATMA GANDHI*
(1869–1948), Indian statesman

In chapter 6, we will examine what it meant when the Christian community proclaimed Jesus as the Son of God, honoring Jesus with divine status because of his resurrection and exaltation. Not only does this designation help explain the close relationship of Jesus and God, but it also clarifies his role as God's messenger, sent into the world to restore it to right relationship with God.

In chapters 7 through 12, we shift our attention from Jesus himself to his public ministry. Chapter 7 explores the goal that focused Jesus' ministry. Jesus proclaimed a new way of relating to God and to others, which he called the kingdom of God. As teacher of this new kingdom way, Jesus dedicated his life in service to God's presence in our world.

Chapters 8 through 10 consider the tasks, roles, and strategies that Jesus the teacher adopted to accomplish his goal of building the kingdom of God. As a prophet, Jesus used

WHAT'S YOUR JQ (JESUS QUOTIENT)? EXPLORING YOUR PERSONAL IMAGE OF JESUS

Here is a brief way to test your IQ about Jesus' identity. This exercise brings to consciousness what you already know about Jesus and highlights some of the ways you imagine him.

Briefly answer the following questions. Often your first impression is more valuable than long reflection. There are no wrong answers.

What do you think Jesus looked like?

How tall was he?
How much did he weigh?
What color were his eyes?
What color was his hair?

Did he have a beard?
Was he muscular?
What were some of his mannerisms?

What is your favorite title for Jesus? For example, what do you call him when you pray?

What is your favorite of Jesus' miracles?

What is your favorite of Jesus' sayings?

What is your favorite of Jesus' parables?

What is your favorite story about Jesus being in controversy with his opponents?

Rank the following descriptions of Jesus from most appealing (1) to least appealing (8):

_____ Lord and Christ

_____ Authoritative teacher

_____ Lord of lords and King of kings

_____ Suffering messiah

_____ New high priest

_____ Saving prophet

_____ God's Son, sent for salvation

_____ Judge of the living and dead

What do you admire most about Jesus?

What do you find most unsettling about Jesus and his message?

If Jesus were sitting across from you now, what one question would you ask him?

Circle the one word in each pair that you think most applies to Jesus as you imagine him.

Gentle	Firm
Humorous	Stern
Reserved	Talkative
Literal	Figurative
Forgiving	Punishing
Impulsive	Cautious
Punctual	Leisurely
Sociable	Detached
Compassionate	Unsympathetic
Passionate	Controlled
Thinking	Feeling
Systematic	Spontaneous
Determined	Hesitant
Critical	Uncritical
Orderly	Careless
Just	Merciful
Calm	Lively
Wary	Trustful
Priestly	Lay
Concrete	Abstract
Jewish	Christian
Active	Passive

parables to teach people how to discover God's presence in their ordinary lives. As a priest, Jesus used the common meal to teach people how to celebrate God's presence. As a king, Jesus offered his wisdom and deeds of power (miracles) to teach people how to reorder their lives around God's presence.

In chapter 11, we look at the significance of Jesus' suffering and death. His death was not accidental but the direct consequence of his claims as Son, his goal of establishing a new kingdom, and his roles as prophet, priest, and king.

In chapter 12, we examine the "good news" of Jesus' resurrection. Had the Gospels ended with his death, they would have not been news, let alone good news for anyone. Jesus' resurrection to new life provided a way for his followers to make sense of his death as God's honorable Son. The indivisible linking of Jesus' life, death, and resurrection is the good news that serves as the foundation of Christian experience and is the source of Christians' hope and the motivation for their mission.

In chapter 13, we recognize that the risen Christ is alive and well and inviting us to follow and to live out the kind of relationship with God and with one another that Jesus taught. The teacher is still inviting seekers to "come and see" and learn from him.

Chapter 14 offers some suggestions about further books that will enhance your knowledge of Jesus and help you continue your search.

The Reader's Guide offers questions for personal reflection and group discussion.

Can anything good come out of Nazareth?

—JOHN 1:46

CHAPTER TWO

Jesus, the Nazarene

As we begin our search for Jesus' identity according to the norms of his culture, we focus on the three most relevant questions that first-century persons would have asked. Is Jesus a male or female? Where is he from? What are his family affiliations? These questions about his gender, geographical location, and genealogy summarize almost everything his ancient neighbors needed to know in order to identify Jesus.

Jesus the Man

In Jesus' world, every child from the moment of birth was set on a culturally determined path because of gender. Males were endowed with honor and granted a privileged status because in that culture males were identified as the normative type of humanity. Females were allotted an inferior status because they were considered to be imperfectly developed males. They were persons whose identity could be granted only in relation to some male, whether a father, spouse, or son. They remained forever identified as daughter of, wife of, or mother of some male.

Males were outwardly oriented toward the public life of the village. They focused their attention on the family fields and village marketplace, on council halls and law courts, and on assemblies where political, social, and economic issues were debated and policies enacted. Females were inwardly oriented toward the household, where the family life, with its childbearing and nurturing, food production and preparation, consumed their energy. Thus men and women lived for all practical purposes in two independently organized worlds that, like two circles, touched only tangentially and seldom overlapped.

Jesus' life, like that of all men in his world, was characterized by public competition. This competition was created by the ancient experience that everything was limited. In today's technically advanced consumer society, we rarely think of anything as having limits. Our answer to any shortfall is merely to produce more.

But in the first century, there was little that technology could do to produce more food, more goods, more security, or more wealth. The limited good, like a giant pie, was all there was. Each family, through its males, scrambled for its share of the pie in order to survive. This situation created a society in which public competition became the essential condition of social existence and survival.

In this first-century culture, a primary value and overriding treasure was honor—one's reputation, recognized and acknowledged by the community, afforded social status and authority. Unlike our culture, in which money or wealth is the dominant value and honor and reputation can be bought, in Jesus' world money could not buy honor.

As a child I received instruction both in the Bible and in the Talmud. I am a Jew, but I am enthralled by the luminous figure of the Nazarene.

—*ALBERT EINSTEIN*
(1879–1955), American physicist and philosopher

Families possessed two types of honor that were distinguished by how the honor came to the family: ascribed (inherited or given as a gift from a benefactor) and acquired. Each type required a different task by the father and the males of the family. Over time, every family accumulated a deposit of both honor and wealth that were bequeathed, protected, and increased from generation to generation.

The result of this social emphasis on competition for the limited goods created a society in which every public interaction between men carried with it the potential for gaining or losing honor for the man and for the family group to which he belonged and represented. Thus every male learned early in life how to participate in this ritualized combat for the limited quantity of honor, power, wealth, and status available in the village.

As a teacher, Jesus gathered to himself a group of like-minded men who formed his band of disciples. Jesus' public teaching, which is described in the four Gospels, was conducted almost exclusively in the public world of men.

Teaching and learning were primarily male domains, and Jesus' teaching was conducted in public—in the synagogue meeting houses, the open fields, along the lakeshore, at meals with other men, in the squares of local villages, and in the temple at Jerusalem—and was usually in dialogue with other males. He seldom appeared in the realm of women (but see John 4:5–27 for his interaction with a Samaritan woman at the town well and his disciples' astonishment). He answered women's questions only as a courtesy because the inferior status of women prohibited them from entering into the public competition of men over honor. Teaching, too, was highly charged with competition. Every question, if it could be answered correctly and cleverly, acquired honor for the teacher. If the teacher could not answer or if he answered poorly, he lost honor and was shown up for his incompetence.

This competitive, contentious attitude was the reason Jesus' opponents constantly tried to bait and trap him into saying something foolish or not answering at all. The Gospels portray Jesus as a teacher with a razor-sharp wit, whose clever answers and memorable one-liners certainly delighted his first-century audience as much as they do us today.

Jesus the Nazarene and Galilean

A person was also closely associated with his or her geographic region. This was especially true in the rural areas, where most people lived in small villages. People with the same name could be easily differentiated by adding their village association. So we have Paul of Tarsus, in Cilicia in southwestern Turkey ("no mean city," Paul brags). We have Mary of Magdala, Joseph of Arimathea, Simon of Cyrene, Nathaniel from Cana in Galilee, and Jesus of Nazareth.

Geographical origin was also a convenient way to categorize strangers. For people who seldom ventured far from their village, distrust of strangers was commonplace. To know someone's geographical origin reduced some of this uncertainty because regional characteristics acted as constants and indicated what typical behaviors to expect. Even today, we have stereotypes of "New Yorkers" or "Texans" or "Americans" associated with their typical behaviors. This labeling reflects the old saying that "when you've seen one, you've seen them all!"

People from particular regions supposedly shared traits and behavior because of the climate and other physical features of their surroundings. Because everyone from a particular place shared the same water, soil, air, and climate, they all would be expected to exhibit the same character traits and behavior. So to know where someone came from provided a stereotype applicable to everyone from there.

Because people's character dictated their behavior, and people from the same region were assumed to act the same way, a person's geographical location was a primary identifier in first-century Palestine. We find this pattern in Paul's letter to Titus, leader of the Christian community on the island of Crete. Paul quotes the proverb that "Cretans are always liars, vicious brutes, lazy gluttons." Then he declares that this is true and urges Titus to expect this kind of behavior and admonish the people appropriately (Ti 1:12–13).

When Jesus began his ministry by inviting the first seekers to follow him, the response of these first disciples set off a kind of chain reaction. Just as John the Baptist had directed his disciples toward Jesus, Andrew rushed off to tell his brother Simon Peter, and Philip told his friend Nathaniel about the fascinating stranger who invited them to follow him.

Like Andrew and Simon Peter, Philip came from the town of Bethsaida on the Sea of Galilee (Jn 12:21), the large inland lake fed by the Jordan River that dominates the region of Galilee in northeastern Palestine. But Nathaniel, who we later learn was from the town of Cana in Galilee (Jn 21:2), about nine miles northwest of Nazareth, did not seem all that impressed with Philip's extravagant suggestion that this man might be the Messiah. Nathaniel seemed even more unimpressed when he heard that the stranger was from Nazareth.

Is it any wonder that to this day this Galilean is too much for our small hearts?

H. G. WELLS
(1866–1946), British novelist

Despite the fact that he had never met Jesus, Nathaniel applied his stereotype of Nazarenes to Jesus. Nazareth's reputation as a no-good village meant Jesus would also be no good. So Nathaniel voiced what must have been the general putdown common to the Galilee region, "Can anything good come out of Nazareth?"

Judging from Nathaniel's reaction, Nazareth must have been a village with an attitude! In the first century, Nazareth was tiny, probably no more than about two hundred and fifty people, many of whom lived in houses partially hewn out of the limestone rocks. This village is not mentioned anywhere in the Old Testament, in the New Testament outside the Gospels, in the writings of the first-century Jewish chronicler Josephus, or in any other first-century writings.

Nazareth had no claim to fame. It was synonymous with obscurity, and if it were not for its most famous native son—who left it finally when unceremoniously rejected by the townsfolk (Lk 4:16–30) and apparently never returned—it would probably still be unknown. But its obscurity was apparently matched only by its reputation for producing nothing of value.

Jesus was always connected with this village of Nazareth. Mark, who narrates nothing about Jesus' early life, implied that Nazareth was Jesus' birthplace by calling it his "hometown" (Mk 6:1). Luke, however, described it as the place where Jesus "had been brought up" (Lk 4:16) rather than as his birthplace, which Luke identified as Bethlehem near Jerusalem (Lk 2:4).

Jesus was also associated with Galilee, the northern frontier of the Jewish homeland. Together with Samaria in the middle and Judea in the south, Galilee was one of the three principal areas of the land of Israel, or Palestine, as it was called by the Romans. Divided into two parts, the rugged mountains of Upper Galilee and the fertile hillsides of Lower Galilee, Galilee's history echoed that of the nation.

A millennium before Jesus' time, Galilee had been the domain of four of the original twelve tribes of Israel. For almost three hundred years it was included in the Northern Kingdom of Israel until it was conquered by the Assyrian armies in 721 B.C. For the next six hundred years, Galilee became inhabited by Gentile foreigners under the domination of its Assyrian, Babylonian, and Greek overlords. In 103 B.C., the Galilean Jewish minority was repatriated when Galilee was conquered by the Jewish Hasmoneans in their drive to carve out an independent state. But in 63 B.C. Palestine once again lost its independence and reverted to the domination of the Romans.

The region of Galilee began about fifty miles north of Jerusalem, which was located in the area called Judea. Because the Jerusalem temple was the only place on earth where God locally dwelt, Jews measured their holiness by the proximity to the temple. In their minds, the closer one was to the center, the more intense was the holiness or contact with God.

Galilee represented a boundary between the heart of Judaism (Jerusalem) and the rest of the (Gentile) world. It was where Jews first encountered Gentiles crossing the borders of their country.

Throughout its history, conquering foreign armies almost always entered Palestine from the north, passing through Galilee and often settling there. Galilee also took on a much more cosmopolitan character because through it ran the main east-west highway from Damascus in Syria to Egypt. Caravans of traders, merchants, and travelers constantly moved through Galilee, multiplying the Jews' commercial contact with Gentiles and their foreign languages and customs.

Thus the region was stereotyped as "Galilee of the Gentiles" (Mt 4:15; 1 Mc 5:15). The word *galilee* means a "circle" or a "district." The image is that of Jews encircled by Gentiles, which is an apt description of this Jewish region ringed by the powerful cities of Acco, Tyre, and Sidon to the west and Damascus and the ten cities of the Decapolis to the north and east.

But for Jews, contact with foreigners produced terrible tensions. From the time of their exile in Babylon (597–538 B.C.), Jews had determined that they would avoid another judgment of God through their careful observance of God's covenant statutes (Torah) in order to become holy, which for them meant being set apart from all others.

For five hundred years they pursued the goal of separatism from other people in order to become a holy people in a holy land with a holy temple. Contact with foreigners who were "unclean," the Jewish way of describing the contamination that obstructed holiness, was always a risky venture and avoided as much as possible. In Galilee, far from the central holiness of Jerusalem, the abundance of Gentile contact was a constant occasion of possible ritual uncleanness.

Boundaries are also places where changes begin. Centuries of political domination and memories of recent freedom under the Hasmoneans planted the seed of hope for a restored Jewish homeland. Thus Galileans were seen as eager to become part of uprisings and revolutions. In the Acts of the Apostles, the famous first-century rabbi Gamaliel recalls the fate of "Judas the Galilean [who] rose up at the time of the census and got people to follow him; he also perished, and all who followed him were scattered" (Acts 5:37).

The climate of Galilee, both physical and cultural, no doubt played a role in Jesus' development and public ministry. Its influence on Jesus is not easy to identify with any certainty. But Jesus does exhibit two characteristics that might be related to the Galilean boundary mentality. Living in closer proximity to Gentiles seems to have created an openness to them that Jews living nearer to Jerusalem did not so readily share. Jesus' openness to Gentiles was carried over to his later followers, as is illustrated by both Peter and Paul in the Acts of the Apostles. Through their leadership, in the course of a few decades the Christian community was transformed from an almost exclusively Jewish group to a predominantly Gentile community.

A second connection to his Galilean roots is Jesus' revolutionary zeal for a new world order. His public teaching is an advocacy for a revolutionary movement unlike any other. He proclaims and builds a kingdom of God, one in which persons would finally return to the original ideal of relationships rooted in love, characterized by justice, and bringing peace for everyone. This kingdom, begun in Galilee, would sweep across the face of the earth.

Jesus' Dubious Honor

Two millennia later it is difficult to tell whether Nathaniel's put-down arises out of his inherent sense of small-village rivalry because, after all, his village of Cana was a lot more impressive (at least in his eyes!) than Nazareth could ever be. But the point of his remark cuts deeper.

Normally, a person's place of origin enhanced one's honorable standing. But in the case of Nazareth in Galilee, there is no measurable honor associated with this village because of its obscurity. Its poor reputation added no significant honor for its native sons but branded them of little value in the eyes of their neighbors.

Being associated with Galilee bestowed no particular honor either. Galileans were from the remote countryside and thus shared none of the sophistication of the city dwellers. For those "big-city" Jerusalemites, Galileans always remained a marginal group from the "boonies," distinguished by such a distinctive accent that even Jerusalem servant girls could recognize it (Mt 26:73). Nathaniel can't believe anything good or anyone honorable, especially God's chosen agent or messiah, could come from such a miserable place as Nazareth. There is too much incongruity between such a lofty claim and such a lowly place. Because honorable deeds were expected to be done by honorable persons, many of Jesus' first-century audience found it hard to connect his honorable reputation with his humble origins.

Jesus' consistent association with Nazareth in Galilee created an irritating tension between his impressive words and deeds and the minimal expectations that people would have had for him. "Where did this man get all this? What is this wisdom that has been given to him? What deeds of power are being done by his hands!" his neighbors ask (Mk 6:2).

But nobody understood this incongruity as well or emphasized it as unmistakably as the men who wrote down Jesus' story. Knowing the Nazareth connection, both Luke and Matthew struggle to explain how Jesus came to be born in Bethlehem so that he could be designated a Davidic messiah.

Jesus' origins in an obscure place that had no status or prestige in the surrounding world contrasted starkly with the claims of messianic kingship that had been made about him and for which he was executed. The Roman governor Pontius Pilate used Jesus' obscure origins as the final insult to the Jewish leaders who sought Jesus' death. Pilate wrote an inscription above the cross that read "Jesus of Nazareth, the King of the Jews." When the leaders protested, Pilate responded, "What I have written I have written" (Jn 19:19–22). To echo Nathaniel, could any real king come from Nazareth?

Jesus, the Descendant of Abraham

In Jesus' world, people had a radically different understanding of human biology and reproduction than we do today. The male was considered the source of life because his "seed" contained a kind of miniaturized version of himself that only needed to be nurtured by depositing it in the fertile ground of a woman's womb.

Once deposited, it would automatically grow into a male child if the conditions of the womb were just right. If the child did not look exactly like the father or if it turned out to be a girl, the causes were traced to variations in the nutrients of the mother's womb rather than any defect in the father's seed.

[Jesus] was not educated at court, as Moses apparently was. He was no son of a king like Buddha. Also he was no scholar and politician like Kung-futse [Confucius], nor was he a rich merchant like Mohammed. Precisely because his origin was so insignificant, his lasting importance is so astonishing.

—*WALTER KASPER*
German theologian and bishop

Because the father was the source of life, bestowing it physically upon his children and socially upon his family, the family's historical existence can be traced through its lists of male ancestors, fathers and sons, whose lineage creates the genealogy as a living testimony to the family's honor. Thus to explain a man's identity is to understand his genealogy.

In the next four chapters, we will examine Jesus' important affiliations, or sonships, noting the groups that Jesus is embedded in, the titles that disclose his honor status, and the roles and expectations that people have of him. Thus we will more fully understand how first-century people might have understood who Jesus was.

TIMELINE OF EVENTS IN THE
FIRST CENTURY OF THE NEW TESTAMENT ERA

37 B.C.: Herod the Great becomes king of Judea

ca. 6–4 B.C.: Jesus of Nazareth is born

4 B.C.: King Herod dies

A.D. 26–36: Pontius Pilate serves as Roman governor in Judea

ca. A.D. 30: Jesus' public ministry begins

ca. A.D. 33: Jesus is crucified in Jerusalem

ca. A.D. 34: Saul (Paul) of Tarsus is converted to the Christian "way"

ca. A.D. 46–49: Paul goes on his first missionary journey

ca. A.D. 49: Apostolic meeting in Jerusalem opens community to Gentiles

ca. A.D. 49–52: Paul goes on his second missionary journey (he begins writing his letters ca. 50)

ca. A.D. 54–57: Paul goes on his third missionary journey

ca. A.D. 58–63: Paul is arrested, sent to Rome for a trial, and imprisoned

A.D. 64: Emperor Nero burns Rome; Christians are blamed and persecuted

ca. A.D. 67: Peter and Paul are martyred under Nero; the apostolic age ends

A.D. 70: Romans destroy the second Jerusalem temple (it is never rebuilt)

ca. A.D. 65–70: The Gospel of Mark is composed

ca. A.D. 70–89: The Gospels of Matthew and Luke are composed

ca. A.D. 95: The exclusion of Christians begins with Pharisaic control of Judaism

ca. A.D. 90–100: The Gospel of John is composed

Is not this the carpenter, the son of Mary?

—MARK 6:3

CHAPTER THREE

Jesus, the Son of Mary and Joseph

Jewish men identified themselves by three significant affiliations. The first was to their immediate family or household; the second, to their clan or extended-family association; and the third, to one of the twelve ancestral tribes of the Israelite people. These tribes originated from the twelve sons of Jacob, or Israel, the grandson of Abraham, the patriarch of the whole Jewish nation. These genealogical affiliations gave a man an "address" within Israel's covenant community.

These same affiliations also identified Jesus to his community. They exhibited his pedigree to others and noted his standing among the people. In this chapter we will explore his affiliation to the "House of Joseph," as the firstborn son of Mary.

The Family in Jesus' Time

Jesus' experience of family was rather different from ours. In a highly structured and status-conscious society in which upward mobility was severely limited, the family was the source of identity and social position, security and economic survival. It included not only blood relatives of the head of the house, but also other dependents—slaves, employees, and any other "clients," that is, freedmen, friends, and others who looked to the head of the house for patronage, protection, or advancement.

The social, economic, and theological realms were bound together and converged on the focal point of the family. Besides long life, a large family was among the most cherished and desirable of God's blessings. It was the essence of God's covenant promise to Abraham (Gn 15:5) and an important reward for obedience to God's covenant guidelines, or law (Lv 26:9; Dt 28:4). Thus barrenness and the death of children were great misfortunes.

The family was the fundamental social and economic unit of society and was rigidly structured by age (hierarchical) and sex (patriarchal). It was central because the whole structure of property ownership and the continuation of the Israelite covenant community rested on the orderly, regular succession of legitimate children from one generation to another. It was also the vehicle through which the religious traditions of the community were passed on to succeeding generations.

Unlike our society, in which families are primarily consumers, in Jesus' world families had to produce many of the necessities of life. All members of the family contributed to the hard work of survival. Children were not considered burdens but gifts to help with the work of the family.

The family was identified as the house of the father. The father, or "patron," embodied the soul, life, and honor (name and reputation) of the family. He was thus responsible for its welfare (provide and protect) and for its continuation by the transmission of new life to children. His role as head of the family was also indicated by distinctive titles signifying his relationship to each of the members: "lord" (husband) to the wife, "father" to his children, "master" to the slaves, and "friend" to those of equal social rank.

That . . . man . . . says women can't have as much rights as man, cause Christ wasn't a woman. Where did your Christ come from? . . . From God and a woman. Man had nothing to do with him.

—*SOJOURNER TRUTH [ISABELLA VAN WAGENER]*
(ca. 1771–1885), to the Women's Rights Conference in Akron, Ohio (1851)

As head of the household, the patron held absolute authority over all who were under his care—wife, children, slaves, hired workers, and guests. He expected respect, submission, obedience, and unquestioning compliance with any

JESUS, THE SON OF MARY AND JOSEPH

of his commands or instructions. He alone could own property and was responsible for providing for and protecting the family. He was the only "adult" in the family, and therefore did the thinking, speaking, and deciding for everyone else.

Wives were dependent, socialized to be submissive to their husband, or "lord." Their primary duty was to manage the household and to provide children to continue the family. Children were socialized to be loyal to the family (uphold its honor and reputation) and to be obedient (to do the will of the father). They were taught to sacrifice their own interests for those of the family. Thus in a hostile and dangerous world they would feel safe only in the family. They would also have what they needed to survive. They were discouraged from taking risks, doing things a new way, showing any independence of mind, or expressing any critical dissent from the ways of the family.

One difference between Christ and other men is this; they do not choose when to be born, but He, the lord and Maker of history, chose His time, His birthplace, and His mother.

—*THOMAS AQUINAS*
(1225–1274), theologian and doctor of the Church

Among the children, males counted more than females. And in the rank or order of children, the firstborn son had priority and certain privileges. Among his siblings, the firstborn son was entitled to a double share of the father's inheritance and would become the next head of the family when the father died. He would also follow in the father's footsteps as head of the family farm or business.

Jesus as Mary's Firstborn

As a son in this family, Jesus shared all the honor and status that the family could bestow. Unfortunately, this honor package was not very large. Nazareth was an obscure village, and its inhabitants were not well born, well educated, or wealthy. Moreover, because the honor scale was based on the holding of land, as a skilled artisan—a carpenter—Joseph would rank rather low.

But within the family Jesus receives a special honor, signified by his designation as Mary's "firstborn son" (Lk 2:7). The firstborn son was considered sacred to God because he opened the mother's womb, the channel of life, to continue the family.

But the firstborn of an Israelite family belonged in a special way to God and had to be redeemed, or bought back, from God with a token sacrifice. And as the firstfruits of the father's seed, the firstborn was thought to be a more exact copy than the children that might follow.

Thus firstborn sons often received preferential treatment and were granted a special relationship with the father. So we discover biblical writers describing how God uses this

41

honorific title of firstborn to identify the people of Israel
(Ex 4:22) and the king, whom God will make "the firstborn,
the highest of the kings of the earth" (Ps 89:27).

What the New Testament Tells Us about Jesus and His Family

If we search through the New Testament, we learn several
details about Jesus and his family. Besides the names of his
parents, we discover that he had brothers and sisters, that
during his ministry they were not closely related nor apparently
very sympathetic with his work, but that after his death at
least one of his brothers played a significant leadership role
in the early church.

However, we must realize that from these scanty bits of
information it is impossible to reconstruct his family situation with any degree of certainty or to answer other questions
that might interest us today. For example, we cannot know
from the scriptural evidence whether these brothers and sisters
were natural or adopted or perhaps even cousins of Jesus.

The Gospels relate that the neighbors from Nazareth
knew Jesus' family well. When Jesus returned to the village
and spoke eloquently in the synagogue, they chided him
for grasping at honors as a teacher and reminded him of his
humble origins. They claimed that this was just Jesus, the
son of Joseph (see, for example, Lk 3:23; 4:22), or the son of
Mary (Mk 6:3), whose brothers and sisters they knew well!

Following the usual patriarchal practice of their culture, the brothers are named (James, Joses or Joseph, Simon, and Judas) but the sisters remain nameless (Mk 6:3; Mt 13:55–56). Jesus' mother and brothers are referred to in each of the Gospel traditions during his public ministry. But they are not counted among his disciples. John sharply differentiates Jesus' disciples from his brothers (Jn 2:12), noting that they do not believe in Jesus (Jn 7:5).

Early in Jesus' ministry, as the rumors about his teaching and healing spread throughout the villages of Galilee, his family became alarmed. They no doubt thought that this adult son's behavior, in particular doing exorcisms and touching lepers to heal them, was damaging his reputation and bringing shame to their family's honor.

So they came to the only logical conclusion: "He has gone out of his mind" (Mk 3:21). Like the townspeople of Nazareth, his mother and brothers thought that Jesus' new teaching and wonder working were not in keeping with his background and station in life. So they came to take him back home.

One can only speculate about the reasons for the tension that might have existed between Jesus and his family during his ministry. But after Jesus' death, the situation with his family changes. Luke includes Jesus' mother and brothers among the 120 faithful believers who huddle for prayer in the upper room awaiting the Pentecost experience of God's Holy Spirit (Acts 1:14).

Paul, whose writings date from the fifties of the first century and antedate the Gospels by some twenty years, remembered his first visit to Jerusalem, around the year 40. On that occasion he met Cephas, or Peter, and "James the Lord's brother" (Gal 1:19), now a leader of the Jerusalem Christian community.

Paul also recalled another meeting fourteen years later with "James and Cephas and John [note that Paul gives prominence to James by mentioning him first, even before Peter!], who were acknowledged pillars" (Gal 2:9) of the Christian community. After a concession speech by James, who speaks for those desiring strict adherence to the Jewish law by Christians, the three pillars offered the handshake of fellowship and blessed Paul's mission to the Gentiles. Paul also noted that "the brothers of the Lord," as distinguished from the apostles and Peter, were active as Christian missionaries and even took their wives along (1 Cor 9:5).

The "Thirty-Something" Jesus

Luke tells us that when Jesus began his public ministry in Galilee, he was "about thirty years old" (Lk 3:23). It was not uncommon for persons in their world to be ignorant of exact birth dates. Thus a designation of "about thirty" not only identifies the chronological time but also hints at the significance of this age. What did it mean to be "thirty-something" in their world?

If Christ is born a thousand times in Bethlehem and not in thee, then are thou lost forever.

—*ANGELUS SILESIUS [JOHANNES SCHEFFLER]*
(1624–1677), mystic and writer, *Cherubic Pilgrim*

It's helpful to understand who actually lived to be thirty-something. In our world a person of thirty is not quite to mid-life (statistically this is closer to 35–39) and is usually in fairly good health. But in Jesus' world, health was always precarious, and life expectancy was much shorter than it is today.

In the first-century world, almost one-fourth of all live births did not survive the first year. One-third of all children who survived infancy were dead by the age of ten. Women married young (twelve was the legal age for Romans), while men married at an older age (fourteen was the legal age but midtwenties was more common because of military service).

Tombstone inscriptions show that the median age of death for wives was thirty-four years and for husbands forty-six years. The dangers connected with childbirth shortened women's life expectancy considerably. Most people did not survive their thirties and only a very few (about 3 percent) would live to age fifty. Old age was not a usual or customary way for people to die. More often death occurred from sickness or accident.

If we relate the age of thirty to the life expectancy of the first century, most men who reached thirty had lived two-thirds of their life and could probably expect to live no more than another decade or so. Thus thirty at that time would be much more like the age of fifty today. This certainly gives a very different picture of Jesus than the one we so often see depicted in movies. Instead of being a young thirty-something wanna-be leader, competing with men ten and twenty years his senior, Jesus was a mature leader whose age and wisdom would immediately command attention and respect from those around him.

Because the ancient people believed that wisdom increased with age, a thirty-year-old Jesus would be a man to listen to and learn from. His knowledge and experience would provide much-needed guidance for his audience, who would have been predominantly younger persons suffering from poor health and without expectations for living more than a decade or two more. To be thirty was to be at the peak of maturity, ready to assume important family, civic, and religious responsibilities.

For the Romans, one's public career usually began at about thirty. Roman men were expected to serve in the military for ten years from the time of their coming of age at about eighteen. After this military experience, they would be ready to begin their careers of public service.

Jesus the Carpenter

As a mature and responsible master and teacher, the thirty-something Jesus takes on the responsibility of building a new community according to God's guidelines. With age comes wisdom, and so he speaks wisely about life and acts with authority because he has lived longer and reflected more than most of his audience has. But he also brings to his task the skills that he has acquired as a master builder, or carpenter.

In the Gospels, the people of Nazareth know Jesus as "the carpenter" (Mk 6:3) and "the carpenter's son" (Mt 13:55). Though "carpenter," that is, a woodworker skilled in doing all kinds of jobs using wood, is the common translation, the Greek word *tekton* (from which we get our word *technical*) designates any skilled artisan and so could mean a "mason" or "smith" (as indeed some of the early fathers of the church took it).

Joseph and Jesus were builders, whose all-purpose skills probably included both carpentry and masonry. Because trade schools did not exist, it was natural for a son to follow in the footsteps of his father, learning the techniques of the family building trade through many hours of apprenticeship. As Jesus once said, "A son cannot do anything on his own, but only what he sees his father doing; for what he does, his son will do also. For the Father loves his Son and shows him everything that he himself does" (Jn 5:19–20, NAB).

But at age thirty, Jesus forsakes his carpentry and begins a new line of work. He applies the skills that he developed as a carpenter to his new vocation to create the kind of ideal community that will live according to God's guidelines. Jesus the carpenter becomes the builder of the kingdom of God.

Satan (tempting Christ):
"Great acts require great means of enterprise,
Thou art unknown, unfriended, low of birth,
A Carpenter thy Father known, thy self
Bred up in poverty and streights at home;
Lost in a Desert here and hunger-bit:
Which way or from what hope dost thou
aspire to greatness?"

—JOHN MILTON
(1608–1674), British poet

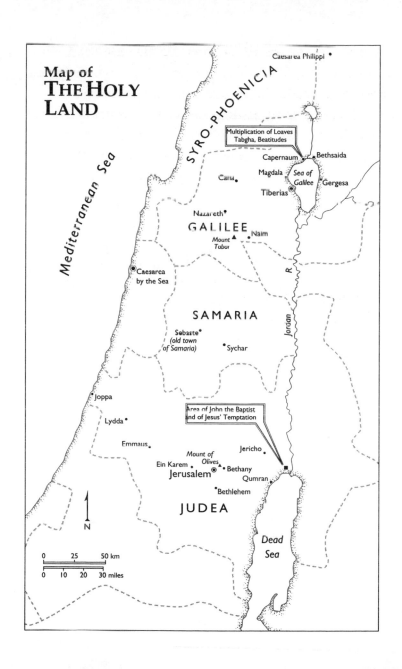

Map of
**THE HOLY
LAND**

SYRO-PHOENICIA

Mediterranean Sea

Caesarea Philippi •

Multiplication of Loaves
Tabgha, Beatitudes

Capernaum • • Bethsaida

Cana • Magdala • *Sea of
Galilee* • Gergesa

Tiberias •

Nazareth •

GALILEE • Naim

Mount
Tabor ▲

Caesarea
by the Sea

SAMARIA

Sebaste •
*(old town
of Samaria)* • Sychar

Jordan R.

• Joppa

Lydda •

Emmaus •

Jericho •

Mount of
Olives ▲
Ein Karem • ◉ • Bethany
Jerusalem • Qumran

• Bethlehem

JUDEA

↑
N

Area of John the Baptist
and of Jesus' Temptation

Dead
Sea

0   25   50 km
0   10   20   30 miles

Are you the one who is to come, or are we to wait for another?

—*MATTHEW 11:3*

CHAPTER FOUR

Jesus, the Jewish Messiah

Besides one's family household, Jewish men identified themselves as Jews, sons of Abraham, and members of a specific tribe and clan within that tribe. Both Matthew and Luke offer genealogies for Jesus that give the reader a kind of honor rating for Jesus. As Matthew makes clear, Jesus' lineage reveals that Jesus is a son of Abraham and son of David (Mt 1:1), that is, an Israelite of the tribe of Judah of the particular clan of David, the great king who unified the twelve tribal peoples into a single kingdom about 1000 B.C.

This information about the ethnic and family affiliations of Jesus reveals that he is not only a Jew but also a member of the royal bloodline of David. Thus Jesus bears proudly his ethnic heritage as a Jew and his royal heritage as a member of the ancient royal family. These bloodlines are extremely important for determining Jesus' honor and are essential for his recognition as the messiah, or anointed one, appointed by God to rule over the people.

What Did It Mean to Be a Son of Abraham?

As a son of Abraham, Jesus is recognized as a member of the covenant family descended from Abraham. Every Jew took pride in being one of the descendants that would be, according to God's promise to Abraham, "as numerous as the stars of heaven and as the sand that is on the seashore" (Gn 22:17). These descendants of Abraham were the people whom God had singled out for a special covenant relationship. To belong to this covenant people was to be a son or daughter of Abraham.

Being a descendant of Abraham was an honor that Jews bore proudly. But Jesus declared that being a member of the covenant people was a privilege that required actions. When some opponents claimed "'Abraham is our father,' Jesus said to them, 'If you were Abraham's children, you would be doing what Abraham did'" (Jn 8:39). Another time, Jesus retorted, "Do not presume to say to yourselves, 'We have Abraham as our ancestor'; for I tell you, God is able from these stones to raise up children to Abraham" (Mt 3:9).

The works of Abraham were summarized in the Jewish law. The law, or Torah, which means "instruction," contained the specific guidelines for the behavior that God demanded of people belonging to the covenant community. By Jesus' time, the written form of this law was contained in the first five books of the Bible (the Pentateuch). By sifting through these books, Jewish scholars identified 613 divine commands summarizing what was required for holy life in their covenant community.

The Gospel writers portray Jesus as very attentive to the demands of Torah. As a Jew, Jesus was circumcised when eight days old to signify his membership in the covenant community (Lk 2:21). As a firstborn, he was redeemed by his parents because he belonged to God (Lk 2:22–24). At thirteen, he became a bar mitzvah—a son of the law—who would be expected to keep the obligations of the covenant encoded in the Jewish law. And in the synoptic Gospels, Jesus is often in controversy with the scholars of the law about the proper interpretation and application of Torah.

What Did It Mean to Be a Son of David?

Besides being an Israelite, Jesus traced his affiliation to the tribe of Judah. When the covenant people had made the Holy Land their own after the exodus from Egypt, the land was allotted according to these ancient tribal divisions. The territory of Judah was that surrounding Jerusalem.

For about seventy years, the twelve tribes were merged into a united kingdom under David and his son Solomon (ca. 1000–930 B.C.). Then ten tribes split off to create the Northern Kingdom of Israel, which lasted until the Assyrian Empire conquered it in 721 B.C. The two remaining tribes, Judah and Benjamin, created the Southern Kingdom of Judah, which lasted until the Babylonian Empire conquered it in 587 B.C. and sent its leading figures into exile. These Judahites, or Judeans, are the clan that gives us the name *Jews*. The collected books of the Old Testament trace the origins and destiny of this southern kingdom.

The Qur'an itself . . . does not only or even most commonly call Jesus a prophet. He is called Messiah eleven times, and many other titles are bestowed upon him. In the Bible John the Baptist was said to be "more than a prophet," and in the Qur'an Jesus is much more.

—*GEOFFREY PARRINDER*
philosopher, theologian of the world's religions

The most prominent clan, or family, of the Judeans was that of David, the great king. The story of his rise from obscurity as a shepherd to become God's anointed king is one of the most exciting and inspiring sections of the Old Testament. After Moses, David was the greatest figure in Jewish history. His personality and his story inspired generations of Jews with the hope of achieving their own political autonomy amidst the major political powers.

After David's death, every king was measured according to his standard. When his dynasty finally collapsed through Babylonian conquest and the people endured fifty years of exile, they hoped to somehow achieve political autonomy with a Davidic descendant once again on the throne. This hope for a new figure that God would send was the root of the messianic hope that burned in the hearts of Jews everywhere.

The people assumed, then, that any new leader of the Jews would be of the "house and family of David" (Lk 2:4). So Jesus began his ministry by choosing twelve followers, whose symbolic meaning reminds us of the twelve tribes David forged into a new nation. Jesus formed these twelve into a new community, which Jesus considered a new Israel. Its guidelines were the Torah, understood according to the directives of Jesus the teacher. Because this new community would finally be the community that God desired, it would usher in the end times.

Like David a millennium earlier, Jesus saw himself as the one chosen and anointed by God to create a kingdom dedicated to life with God. The word *anointed* (Hebrew, *messiah*, or Greek, *christos*) was the specific title that identified Jesus' royal affiliation and honor. The identifier *Christ* became so closely connected with Jesus that for Christians it is practically his last name.

What Did the People Expect in a Messiah?

Awaiting the Messiah expressed the enduring Jewish hope for God to enter history and deliver them once again as God had done with the Exodus from Egypt. Jews realized that their whole history was the story of God's continual deliverance. When their situation became desperate, God could enter either directly (as with Abraham) or through chosen intermediaries (Moses, the charismatic judges, David and the kings, prophets, priests, and wise teachers). The divine appointment of these agents was signified by an anointing with oil or with God's own Holy Spirit.

During the Jewish experience in the millennium and a half before Christ, the people's expectations of a messiah shifted as the nation's circumstances changed. The major events around which their national memory was focused were the Exodus, the kingdom, the Exile, and the restoration. These experiences provided the groundwork for their worldview, their theology, and their national life. They also demonstrate to us how God provided messianic deliverers who were tailored to the needs of the situation.

God as Deliverer

The original liberator, of course, was God. From out of the blue, as we say, God appeared suddenly to Abraham. Abraham's difficult situation was that he was landless and childless. God had already allotted the whole earth to the nations, but

Abraham had no land to call his own. Moreover, approaching ninety, he had never had children to carry on his family name and tradition. Then God entered directly into Abraham's life (Gn 12:1–3), promising innumerable descendants (Gn 22:17) and a land in which they could dwell as God's own chosen people (Gn 15:1–21).

Moses as Prophet

Five hundred years later, the chosen people were in Egypt, mired in slavery. To rescue them, God chose Moses, the great mediator between God and the people. Moses was the archetype of a prophet, or spokesman, for God. God spoke to him "face to face" (Ex 33:11) and he conveyed the words of God to the people (Ex 19:1–20:21). He was also the model of the type of leader God wanted for the people.

This rescue, or exodus, of the Hebrews from domination by the most powerful empire of that time signaled God's fulfillment of the promise made earlier to Abraham: they would have a land of their own. It also solidified the covenant relationship between God and the people. God was their deliverer; therefore, the people were obligated to live as God desired and instructed. On their way to the Promised Land, the people were given their instructions for living, from God through Moses. The Mosaic covenant law remained the foundation for all later forms of Jewish life. Moses' example became the model for all Jews to emulate.

A Spirit-Empowered Judge

Although the people thought they had received their land grant from God, they had to fight to oust the previous inhabitants in order to enter and settle the land. They also needed to protect themselves from the residual hostility of neighboring peoples who remembered their displacement and were on the lookout to find a way to reclaim their land.

The political organization of the people for the first two hundred or so years after entering the Promised Land was as a brotherhood of tribes rather than as a hierarchical empire. The Hebrews understood that they had been chosen because God wanted them to be a society different from all the neighboring peoples. But whenever there was trouble, God provided Spirit-filled leaders, called judges—such as Deborah, Barak, Gideon, and Samson—to rescue them from the threats of their enemies (Jgs 2:13–19; 4:1–5:31; 6:1–8:32; 13:1–16:31).

An Anointed King

But around the turn of the millennium, the people wanted a king like other nations had (1 Sm 8:1–22). Strong opponents recognized that having a human king would change the dynamics of this chosen community. It would also threaten God's sovereignty as their only king. The tension of this choice runs throughout the story of the kings of Israel and Judah.

The compromise seems to have been that the people could have a king but God had to be the one who chose him, and he would rule according to the guidelines of the Torah. And even a chosen king, Saul for example, could go out of favor with God, and a new king, David, would receive the divine approval and reign in God's place (1 Sm 16:1–13; 2 Sm 7:7–14). Because God's choice was confirmed by anointing with oil, the king was God's anointed one (1 Sm 10:1–7).

A Spirit-Anointed Prophet

When the Hebrew tribes became a kingdom, prophets also appeared. They were not anointed with oil but rather with the Spirit of God (Is 61:1–3). This irresistible divine power urged them to speak God's word to the people no matter what the cost.

These prophets speak as God's intermediaries to the king and the people. In the rough-and-tumble world of power politics, rulers tended to identify what was good for the nation with their own interests and to rely on their own wisdom and power to rescue the nation from potentially disastrous situations. The prophets spoke on behalf of God in the difficult situations confronting the nation, reminding the people of God's agenda and encouraging trust in God rather than in human power and wisdom.

The prophets constantly warned about what would happen if the people were not faithful to God by keeping their part of the covenant. And in 587 B.C. the last of the chosen people were conquered by the Babylonian Empire. The temple

in Jerusalem was destroyed and many of the people were
exiled to Babylon.

An Anointed Priest

In most ancient empires the king was the sole representative
of God—warrior, judge, prophetic spokesman, and priest.
But from the time of Moses, the Hebrews separated the
functions of priest, prophet, and king. Moses' brother, Aaron,
assumed the priestly role for worship in the movable holy
tent on their journey through the wilderness to the Promised
Land (Ex 28:1–3; 40:13). His descendants continued this role
when the kings built a temple in Jerusalem in which God
could dwell on earth (see, for example, 1 Kgs 3:1; 5:15–19;
6:1–38).

The temple was the only place on earth where God
physically dwelt, and so it was the center of Judaic life. We
cannot imagine the trauma that ensued when the Babylonians
destroyed this temple and forced the Jews to confront the
haunting questions: Was God really not there? Wasn't God
powerful enough to protect himself from the Babylonian
deities? Didn't God care anymore? Was this the final sign that
their covenant relationship had ended?

Throughout the fifty years of exile, the priests and scribes
pondered these agonizing questions. They sifted through
their scriptures looking for clues. Ezekiel, the visionary prophet,
was visited in exile by God riding on a moving chariot-throne

(Ez 1). Isaiah proclaimed that God would indeed restore the people (Is 49:8–23). After Cyrus the Great of Persia defeated Babylon to become the new world emperor, he decreed in 538 B.C. that the exiles could return.

The Christ had to suffer and die, because whenever the Divine appears in all Its depth, It cannot be endured by men.... In the picture of the Crucified, we look at the rejection of the Divine by humanity.

PAUL TILLICH
theologian, Shaking the Foundations

Upon their return, the first item on the agenda was rebuilding the temple. This second temple, which would be in continual updating until the time of Jesus, would last until A.D. 70, when it was destroyed by the Romans. Since that date the Jews have had no central temple, and all of the rites and ceremonies that were to go on at that temple have never been performed. What Jews call a temple today refers to a synagogue and not the temple in Jerusalem. And synagogue worship is not the same as the temple worship as specified in the Old Testament—sacrifices of animals, grain, incense, and so forth. Only the Passover, which was not celebrated in the temple but in the family, still continues today according to the ancient ritual guidelines.

The second item was the revising of their sacred writings. The true story of their relationship with God was now clear. Exile did not mean the end. Restoration—deliverance and rescue—not judgment, was God's final word to them. The pattern of broken relationship (sin) and divine rescue (salvation) was now understood as the pattern of their covenant relation to God. So they refashioned their scriptures to highlight this underlying pattern. This postexilic revision is the Old Testament that we have today.

The third item on the agenda was to live in such a way that the Exile would never happen again. The priests recognized that the Exile had served as a punishment for their sins. So the priests set out to ensure that the lifestyle of the people would be holy, that is, set apart from all others.

For the next five hundred years, this "holiness agenda"— to be a holy people, in a holy land, worshiping in a holy temple—characterized the Jewish people. They set themselves apart from others by emphasizing circumcision as the sign of their covenant membership, by following a strict diet, by limiting intermarriage with non-Jews, and by displaying a fanatic loyalty to their God, not just as one God among many but as the only God.

What Would the Ideal Messiah Be Like?

A millennium before Jesus, the tiny kingdoms of Israel and Judah could come into existence and remain independent only during a time when the world political climate was favorable. Egypt to the south was teetering in its old age, and the empires that would dominate the area for centuries—Assyria, Babylonia, Persia, Greece, and Rome—had not yet embarked on their paths of world conquest. But from 721 B.C. to the time of Christ, as each empire took its turn at world domination, first Israel and then Judah became their vassals. When political freedom slipped away, the people's hopes for a divinely chosen rescuer increased.

This hope for a new messiah sent by God became the hope for an ideal deliverer. This ideal messiah incorporated aspects of the many types of deliverers that God had already sent. Some wanted a renewed covenant experience and expected a prophet like Moses who would renew the familiarity they had once had with God. Others wanted political freedom and yearned for a warrior-king like David who would create an independent Jewish state. Still others wanted a priestly figure who would finally fulfill the holiness agenda and achieve the covenant ideal.

But no matter what type of messiah was envisioned, his appearance was connected to a persistent hope that God would usher in a new time when the present evils and inequalities would end. Everyone hoped for a "new creation," where our disordered would be reordered by God into its original, mint condition. Then the chosen people, like Adam and Eve in Eden, would live as God intended—without work, without pain, without sin, sickness, and death. God's messianic agent would bring this new heaven to earth.

Messianic Surprises: Jesus the Christ

At the time of Jesus, the people of Palestine had been languishing for almost a century under the domination of the Roman Empire and for almost forty years under the Herod family, whose commitment to Judaism was suspect but whose allegiance to Rome was not. Any yearning for freedom pictured the rescuer as one sent from God according to the types of agents already experienced in Jewish history. So when people began to envision Jesus as a messiah, the one whom God had promised to bring about their liberation, he was understood against the backdrop of these historical figures.

Being identified as the Messiah was central to the understanding of Jesus, not only by his followers but also by his enemies. It was over this title that he was tried, convicted, and crucified. This title became the primary rallying cry of his disciples after his death, and so synonymous with Jesus as to become like his last name. He is no longer Jesus the Christ but simply Jesus Christ.

But it is clear that none of these messianic descriptions exactly fit Jesus and his work. The Gospel writers indicated that he was a divinely appointed agent by his Spirit-filled anointing at baptism. When he asked his disciples, "Who do you say I am?" Peter identified him as the Messiah (Mt 16:13–20; Mk 8:27–30; Lk 9:18–21). Jesus accepted this title, but he modified it to specify the particular way that he understood his messianic role to include his suffering, death, and then resurrection to new life. It was not one that focused on glory, but rather on service. And the highest form of service was to give one's life for others (Mk 10:45; Rom 5:6–8).

Jesus did not accept the profile of any preconceived messianic figure without modification. Whenever he was identified as Messiah, he accepted the title but added further dimensions to indicate the way he was filling the role. He was in some ways a prophet like Moses. Matthew hinted at the parallels in the way Jesus was saved as a child, fled with his family to Egypt, and returned to bring the people together by teaching a new law. He was also cast in the mold of the prophets Elijah, whom some thought he was (Mt 16:14; Mk 6:15; 8:28; Lk 9:8, 19), and Elisha. The signs and wonders of these two prophets (healing, multiplying bread, bringing the dead to life, etc.) were similar to those performed by Jesus (1 Kgs 17:9–24 on Elijah; 2 Kgs 4:1–5:19 on Elisha).

Jesus is the Black Christ! . . . By becoming a black man, God discloses that blackness is not what the world says it is. . . . The Black Christ is he who threatens the structure of evil as seen in white society, rebelling against it, thereby becoming the embodiment of what the black community knows it must become.

—*JAMES H. CONE*
theologian

Because being a priest demanded that one be a member of Aaron's clan, Jesus was disqualified from any formal priestly role. But he assumed the priestly task of sacred service, facilitating communion with God. Jesus, however, did not think temple worship and rituals were the primary way to please God. He adjusted the definition for holiness. It no longer meant being separate from everyday life; it meant being immersed in everyday life because God was present there.

But the major revision Jesus brought to the perception of "messiah" was his refusal to save the people by political revolution or violence. Jesus' reluctance to accept the profile of a messiah as a national political hero, who would liberate the Jews from their Roman overlords by rebellion, distanced Jesus from the Jews who formed the zealot faction that yearned for a war of liberation in which God would step in to save them. In fact, in the year A.D. 66 they would indeed incite a war with Rome. Expecting God's intervention, the zealots were profoundly discredited when the war turned ugly and the wrath of Rome was unleashed on God's temple, razing it to the ground in the year 70. It has never been rebuilt.

The Christian identification of Jesus as the expected messiah was also influenced by their belief that with Jesus the final age of the world had begun. To understand this dimension of his messianic role, Christians applied the characteristics of the Old Testament description of one like a "son of man" who would be the bearer of the new age.

Who is this Son of Man?

—*JOHN 12:34*

CHAPTER FIVE

Jesus, the Bearer of the New Age

What is meant by the phrase *son of man*? Scholars believe that it stems from the very early Christian understanding of Jesus, which was rooted in Judaism. But this title occurs almost exclusively in the Gospels, and then only on the lips of Jesus. And although it plays a very prominent role in the Gospels as a way of understanding Jesus, it then seems to vanish from the Christian vocabulary and receives little attention in later theology or liturgy.

"Son of" or "daughter of" was a common way in Semitic languages to designate an individual member of a group. So Jewish priests were all "sons of Aaron" (see, for example, Lv 3:13), heavenly beings were "sons of heaven," women were "daughters of humans" (Gn 6:4), and the women who lived in Jerusalem were "daughters of Jerusalem" (Lk 23:28).

In the Old Testament (which shaped the religious meanings in Jesus' culture), a "son of man" identified a human person, especially in contrast to God. But this title takes on a particularly important meaning for Christians because in the book of the prophet Daniel it describes the final agent God will send to bring God's rule to the world.

Son of Man as a Human Being

The title "son of man" appears frequently throughout the Old Testament to designate a human being as distinct from God. It is especially prominent in the book of Ezekiel (as is clear in the NAB version), where God addresses Ezekiel frequently as "son of man," meaning "you human being." This designation constantly highlights the contrast between humanity and divinity.

But if we move beyond this general information about the title to note that it also confers an honor, then this title is not a simple designation of Jesus' humanity. There was no need to claim this. In the earliest Christian literature there was never a doubt about whether Jesus existed or was human. The question was whether he could be something more than human.

Only Jesus used this title for himself, which suggests that he chose the title. It could be that it expressed for him the honor of being human. It's more likely that Jesus chose this

title for what it meant in the prophetic book of Daniel—
a book that, as a faithful Jew, Jesus would have been very
familiar with.

Son of Man as God's Final Envoy

Christians expanded their belief that Jesus was the Davidic
messiah by connecting that figure with the one described by
Daniel as "one like a son of man" who was to be God's final
envoy, or agent, for the transformation of the world.

Daniel's stunning vision of God's final coming into our
history was very familiar to the early Christian community.
Its familiarity could very likely be traced to Jesus' self-
description as *the* Son of man because he saw himself and
his work as the fulfillment of Daniel's prophecy.

He was made human so that we might be made divine.

—*ATHANASIUS*
(ca. 296–373), bishop of Alexandria, *De Incarnatione*

Daniel's majestic vision described the coming of God's
agent for the final judgment and deliverance of the world
from the disorder caused by sin and the domination of Satan,
the evil one. For biblical writers, human empires with their
arrogance and pride constituted the prime example of a
disordered cosmos.

Daniel saw a vision of the kingdoms that ruled over the earth, pictured imaginatively in the succession of four ferocious beasts representing the world-dominating empires of Egypt, Assyria, Babylon, and Greece. The beasts of these empires are all composite and mixed hybrids rather than the pure forms of animals that God created.

We could never recognize the Father's grace and mercy except for our Lord Jesus Christ, who is a mirror of His Father's heart.

—MARTIN LUTHER
(1483–1546), Reformation Scripture scholar and theologian, *Catechism*

Their domination, in opposition to the domination of God from heaven, is broken when final dominion is given to one who is not a beast but is rather in human form, "one like a son of man" (Dn 7:13, NAB). Christians, of course, identified this figure with the risen Lord Jesus, who was God's image and incarnation in human form. Thus he was not just "a son of man" but "*the* Son of man."

From the Exodus onward, whenever God broke into history to oppose the false domination of empires, God's intervention followed the judgment/salvation pattern. God first judged the wicked, in particular idolaters who lacked the proper loyalty and commitment to God, then saved those who remained loyal, especially those who endured hardships on account of their faith commitment. The God who had expelled evil from the heavenly realm would then purify our earth. God's justice and judgment on all nations and empires were the price they paid for giving their loyalty and worship to Satan.

Christians believed that the struggle between God and Satan for domination of the earth was decisively won by Jesus' death and resurrection. Jesus was the final agent of God's judgment and salvation. Now God's judgment of all evil empires would be carried out, beginning with the fall of the current evil empire, Rome. The downfall of this mightiest of empires would usher in the final restoration of the entire earth as a kingdom ruled by God and ordered with the harmony God intended at its creation.

Jesus as the Son of Man

The Christian use of this title might well have been rooted in the actual way that Jesus used the ambiguous term *son of man* to describe himself and his solidarity with all humanity. This might have been the title of honor that Jesus chose for himself, which would explain why it always appears on his lips throughout the Gospel accounts.

But Jesus added further meanings by connecting the Son of man with the suffering that was part of his messianic task (see, for example, Mk 8:31) and the forgiveness of sins (Mt 9:6; Mk 2:10; Lk 5:24), which the Jews believed only God could do. Thus the title could point to him as just another human person, or as the suffering, sin-forgiving savior, or finally, as the triumphant eschatological figure brandishing the power of God for the kingdom. Because "the son of man" could have these different meanings, Jesus' audience had to decide which meaning he was using.

Connecting the Layers of Jesus' Identity as the Son of Man

For Christians, Jesus was the expected messianic agent who also had a task related to the final transformation of the world. The Messiah was not just the liberator, a political leader on the throne of David, but the final envoy who ushered in God's ultimate transformation of our sinful world into the kind of world God envisioned before sin disrupted it. Most of the passages that call Jesus the Son of man are describing him as one who forgives sins, saves, heals, and performs miracles. They also liken Jesus to the suffering servant in the Old Testament book of Isaiah, which we will consider in chapter 11 where we examine the meaning of Jesus' suffering and death.

As with all of his titles, Jesus' identity as the Son of man takes on a unique spin. Jesus makes his personal modifications to this title just as he did to all the others. Jesus accepts the title Son of man and the honor that goes with it. He is both a human being and God's final agent, but in a unique way through his suffering. Thus Jesus as the Son of man draws together several dimensions of his identity.

Human being. Jesus is certainly a human being—a physical son, or "child." His humanity was self-evident and never something that people argued about. He was obviously human, even to the point of suffering and dying a shameful death by crucifixion. Jesus' designation as Son of man, or human being, could have become more important for his later followers as they began to affirm his divine status. Thus the title would be a reminder of his solidarity with all humanity.

Messianic king. Jesus was also the promised messianic "king," exercising God's rule over the earth. The book of Revelation, composed approximately sixty years after Jesus' death, aptly summarizes this divine dominion. "Then the seventh angel blew his trumpet, and there were loud voices in heaven, saying, 'The kingdom of the world has / become the kingdom of our Lord / and of his Messiah, / and he will reign forever and ever'" (Rv 11:15). But the coming of the Messiah was not necessarily the beginning of God's final transformation of the world.

God's final envoy. As God's final envoy, or messenger, the Son of man shares the divine power that will usher in God's kingdom. Thus the Son of man participates in the divine actions of forgiving sins, judging people's actions, and performing deeds of power.

One who suffers. But no matter how important and high his status was, Jesus was distinguished from all other messiahs and divinely sent agents as the one who suffers. Jesus the Son of man is directly associated with the suffering-servant role that Christians fastened upon to explain the meaning of his suffering. Hence many texts refer to the Son of man as one who must suffer.

One who is glorified. The final dimension of the Son of man title recognizes that the Son of man will be glorified by God as a reward for his service as God's agent. This is the key link to the belief that Jesus is divine. According to Christian belief, Jesus, after he is raised from the dead, is honored by being seated at God's right hand, sharing God's glory and worship.

To worship Christ as God brings him into the realm of divinity. As God's divinely chosen agent, and as ruler of the world (as judge, savior), Jesus shares God's powers over creation (miracles) and so shares the honor and glory attributed to divinity. The final step is to share God's honor and divine identity. This divinity will be expressed by the title *Son of God,* recognizing that Jesus belongs to the group of divine beings.

From Being the Divine Agent to Being Divine

By connecting the attributes associated with God in Daniel's vision, the Gospel writer John suggested that Jesus, the "son of man" in Daniel's vision, was divine. Because Jesus shared these divine characteristics, the intended conclusion was that he must also be divine. Because Jesus was divine and shared God's power, he could do what God could do. Jesus' divine identity spilled over into a description of what Jesus did as God's chosen agent.

This Son of man designation was the key step in moving from an understanding of Jesus as human to associating Jesus with divinity through the title *Son of God.* But as we will see, even this Son of God title took on a new meaning when it referred to the unique relationship of Jesus to God.

It is to the humble-minded that Christ belongs, not to those who exalt themselves above his flock. . . . The Lord Jesus Christ did not, for all his power, come clothed in boastful pomp, and overweening pride, but in a humble frame of mind.

—CLEMENT
(ca. A.D. 96), bishop of Rome

Perhaps this movement by his followers to the proclamation of his divine status as Son of God is why the Son of man title eventually lost its importance in Christian teaching. First of all, it is a Semitic term that would have less meaning when the church turned its attention to the Gentiles.

However, because of its roots in Jesus' ministry and preaching, it was retained in the Gospel traditions, and it recalled the first Christians' struggle to explain who Jesus was.

In addition, Son of man was a transitional term. Once the final destination was reached, namely belief in Jesus' divine status, then the importance of this transitional link was no longer necessary. New converts began with an affirmation of Jesus' divinity as the Son of God, as Lord and Christ. This highest honor thus subsumed all others, and the difficult process of getting to this designation was forgotten. Once Christians affirmed Jesus as Christ, the Son of God, the Son of man title had done its work to reveal that God's final agent was not just the Messiah but more precisely God's own Son who suffered and was glorified.

They should have known he was a God. His patience should have proved that to them.

—TERTULLIAN
(ca. 160–225), African theologian and apologist

Are you, then, the Son of God?

—*LUKE 22:70*

CHAPTER SIX

Jesus, the Son of God

The affirmation that Jesus was the Son of man was the key link to the Christian claim that Jesus was more than a human being. But this claim did not yet clearly express the belief that Jesus, who through his suffering and death would finally bring in the end times, was more than merely God's agent for justice. This step was taken when Christians identified Jesus as the Son of God.

Keeping in mind how patriarchal that culture was and how critical a person's title was in the community, it's not difficult to understand the type of honor that accompanied the identification as God's Son. This title and claim were common in the ancient Near Eastern culture. However, the Christian claim of Jesus being God's Son went beyond any other use of that title.

Types of Sonship

In the ancient world, as today, there were two types of paternity, natural (Latin, *natus,* meaning "born," hence, by generation or "blood") and social (legal, by adoption or "bond"). Both forms were important and common. But whether one was a son by generation or by adoption, the social implications in the eyes of the community were the same. The affiliation to the family and the honor that went with it were publicly recognized by all.

Like everything else in Jesus' society, women's wombs were a limited commodity. The primary goal of marriage was not sex but the survival of the family through the generation of children.

The father of a family guarded his women and their wombs so that no other male might sow his seed there. This was absolutely essential if a father was to make sure that his children were really his own. There was seldom a doubt about who the mother of a child was (but see 1 Kgs 3:16–28 for the wisdom of King Solomon when maternity was disputed). But unless the womb of the wife had been kept protected, there could always arise questions about who the father was. Thus even a natural child had to be socially claimed by the father as his own for the child's honor to be recognized by the community.

By acknowledging the newborn child as his own through naming and claiming, the father of the family confirmed his paternity to the community in a way that transcended natural considerations. This practice of social confirmation also appeared in the adoption formula that made a child a full member of the family. In a world in which families often lacked natural heirs, the practice of adoption, especially of sons, was common. Through adoption, the father bestowed all the legal rights and social privileges that a natural child would have.

Christ is God or He is the world's greatest impostor.

—*DOROTHY DAY*
American social reformer, *From Union Square to Rome*

So to determine the meaning of a claim of sonship, we must recognize that it could be understood either as adoption or as natural generation. But whether by blood or by bond, in the eyes of the community the affiliation to the family group and a male's social status and honor as a son were exactly the same.

Sons of God: Kings and the Chosen People

In the ancient Near East, the designation "son of God" was common for royalty, but it was always thought of as resulting from adoption. In Egypt the pharaoh was considered God's son and hence a god too. Alexander the Great, as he moved eastward in his conquests, also became enamored of this divine honor and the worship that went with it. By the time of Jesus, the Roman emperors had begun to declare themselves divine.

The title *son of God* expressed the claim of a close relationship between God and the king. In society as a whole, the king was different from all others in status and honor, social prestige and power. The king represented God to the people and was the channel through which God's benefits trickled down to the people.

The king was God's son in that he was the representative of God on earth, and so wielded power and authority as if he were God. But the more one was treated "as if" he were a god, the greater the danger that he would actually begin to believe himself a god. There were lots of sons of God by adoption, but few claimed sonship by divine generation.

The Catholic Church lives and goes forward by this faith that in Christ Jesus there is neither humanity without true divinity nor divinity without true humanity.

—*POPE LEO THE GREAT*
(390–461)

It was one thing for Greek mythical heroes like Castor or Pollux to be born of the union of Zeus and a woman, but real historical individuals did not usually have the luxury of such grandiose claims. Their parents were far too ordinary to produce such a marvelous offspring whose actions benefited all humanity. Another problem arose when these "divine" kings died. If God were their real father, then they would not die—or, like Jesus, they would die and then rise to new life as one of the immortals!

The title *son of God* was also found within Israel. Several of the royal psalms, which scholars think might have their origin and function in coronation ceremonies that included anointing, identify the king as God's son. Psalm 2:7 provides an adoption formula in which God designates the king as his son: "You are my son; today I have begotten you."

However, "son of God" designated not just the king, but the whole people because God was understood as the father of Israel (see, for example, Tb 13:4). But again, this honor title was rooted in the claim of a distinctive relationship that set apart the Israelites from other peoples in the surrounding cultures. Israel was God's people, his firstborn, not by natural procreation but by adoption.

Jesus' Divine Sonship: Adoption or Generation?

The designation *son of God* thus associated one intimately with God. In particular, it identified one who shared God's power and so acted toward others the way God would. Thus a king who bestowed great benefits on others, someone who did great deeds to provide or protect the nation or city, would be a likely candidate for this title.

Because Jesus was perceived as one who not only exhibited the divine power at work in his wondrous deeds of healing and exorcism but also brought the greatest benefit of salvation to all humanity, it was natural to move toward thinking about him as a son of God.

If Jesus was truly the Son of God, then either he was "made" God's Son (by designation, similar to the process of adoption) or he was born God's Son (by conception or natural generation).

We can note, however, that within the early Christian writings, there was a development in how Jesus' sonship or affiliation with God was understood and explained. The initial understanding of Jesus as God's Son by adoption soon changed into a claim that Jesus was God's Son by natural generation. This latter direction introduced a striking claim that went beyond any claim made by Roman emperors or oriental potentates. This claim of divine status and honor demanded more sophisticated explanations.

Mark's Gospel, which tells nothing about Jesus' birth or youth, depends upon the first alternative and presents a claim of adoption. Luke and Matthew, however, follow the second alternative and claim a unique generation for Jesus through the power of God's Holy Spirit. John's Gospel introduces a surprising third alternative that claims Jesus was divine from eternity, even before anything was created, and was sent into our world to bring salvation and then return to heaven.

Adoption Formula: Jesus Made Son of God

Thinking about how Jesus is "made" God's Son by adoption means that there is no question of a natural generation. Jesus was as human as we are. Mark's Gospel contains no stories of Jesus' birth or childhood but begins when Jesus was an adult.

After a brief introduction that sets the story of Jesus within the Old Testament matrix of prophecy and the hope for a promised messiah, Mark begins with the baptism of Jesus. As Jesus came out of the water, a voice from heaven, which of course can be none other than God, uses the terminology of an adoption formula to affirm Jesus as God's beloved Son (Mk 1:11). The language of Mark's adoption formula echoes God's adoption of an Israelite king as his beloved child (Ps 2:7). Later in the Gospel, after Jesus reveals that he must suffer as part of God's plan for salvation, the same voice is heard again reaffirming this loving relationship (Mk 9:7).

God's adoption bestowed the highest honor and dignity on Jesus. Adoption was not something that one could do for oneself but depended upon the free choice of a father and was one of the most significant benefits or gifts that any patron could bestow.

Only God can make one a son of God. To assume this honor and this title for oneself is to step beyond the bounds of right relations and commit the greatest act of insolence. To grasp at honors rather than receive them from a patron as a gift exhibits the most shameful behavior. No wonder the Jews refused to acknowledge this honor claim of Jesus and thought he should die for claiming such an honor on his own. As the Jews explained to Pilate, "We have a law, and according to that law he ought to die, because he made himself the Son of God" (Jn 19:7, NAB).

The rest of Mark's Gospel is organized in such a way as to confirm Jesus' honor as adopted Son of God. The reader is led to remember that despite the humiliations and degrading suffering and crucifixion, Jesus was really the Son whom God loved and would vindicate. Thus the gift of new life by resurrection was the result and reward of God's love for this Son.

Adoption by God establishes an affiliation with God. This affiliation is as close as that of a natural father and son and is a sharing of the power and mission, honor and praise, respect and worship that is accorded the Father. So from the moment of Jesus' baptism, he was declared to be God's beloved Son with all the rights and privileges of a natural child.

Generation Accounts: Jesus Born as Son of God

Interestingly enough, both Matthew and Luke revise Mark's version of the Gospel by adding stories about the birth of Jesus that change the claim of sonship from adult adoption to natural generation. They do this because in the five to fifteen years between Mark's Gospel (written about A.D. 70) and theirs, the claim that Jesus was the Son of God under went a major change within the community of believers.

The infancy narratives attempt to persuade readers of Jesus' divine sonship by narrating events that are in keeping with Jesus' divine designation. Composed forty years or more after Jesus' death, these infancy narratives express the significance of Jesus and his life written back into his childhood. To understand these infancy narratives and their role in the gospel, we must recall first that the ancients had no developmental view of the human person. The child was considered to be a miniature version of its adult form. Children dressed in smaller versions of adult clothes and for the most part were expected to act like adults. This was still the case until about a century ago when an understanding of childhood and adolescence began to develop.

Second, because everyone's childhood was insignificant and obscure, the childhood of great figures was understood by taking their adult character and accomplishments and simply scaling them down to the childhood level. Thus in Luke's Gospel, we find the twelve-year-old Jesus hanging out in the temple in dialogue with the great Jewish teachers of his day. This prefigures what he would be doing later in his life as a renowned teacher.

Thus the infancy narratives convey the same truths about Jesus but express them in the events of his birth. Because the

Gospel writers believed that the Jesus was the Son of God, they read this honor back into the circumstances of his birth.

Although Matthew and Luke work independently of each other, their strategy is remarkably similar. They are primarily concerned with the theological claim that Jesus was God's Son by natural generation and indicate his divine sonship in several ways. Jesus' unique relation to God is revealed in the circumstances surrounding his unique birth. Both Gospel writers stress that God alone was responsible for this child in a way that went beyond God's normal gift of a child through the sexual intercourse of the parents.

In the eyes of the community, Jesus was the son of Joseph and Mary. However, both Matthew and Luke indicate in their birth accounts and in their genealogies that Joseph was not the natural father of Jesus. Through the power of the Holy Spirit (the divine principle of life), God alone, not Joseph, supplied the "seed" for Jesus that was nurtured in Mary's womb. Luke wrote that Mary was a virgin and had not had sexual relations with Joseph (Lk 1:26–38). Matthew narrated that Mary was already pregnant and Joseph knew that this was not his child (Mt 1:18–23). With God's help, Joseph was persuaded to take Mary as his wife and adopt Jesus as his son.

Moving from fathers to sons, Matthew traces the genealogical roots of "Jesus the Messiah, the son of David, the son of Abraham" (1:1). He begins with Abraham and organizes the genealogy into three groupings of ancestors related to the stages of the growth of the Israelite people. Each generation is indicated by the formula identifying the ancestor as "the father of" the child.

When Matthew finally gets to Joseph, from the pattern we expect him to say "Jacob the father of Joseph, Joseph the father of Jesus." But he changes the long chain of ancestors to say very precisely "Jacob the father of Joseph the husband of Mary, of whom Jesus was born" (1:16). Thus Matthew carefully brings his genealogy into compliance with his claim that Jesus was God's natural Son, not Joseph's.

Luke traced the ancestry of Jesus as Son of God in the opposite direction, working his way backward from son to father. But he also offered a subtle clue to remind his readers about Jesus' divine sonship. Luke began the genealogy by noting that what people thought did not conform to the reality. Jesus "was the son (as was thought) of Joseph" (3:23), which brings the genealogy into conformity with the first two chapters of his Gospel, which maintained that Jesus was not the natural son of Joseph but the unique Son of God, born from the virginal womb of Mary.

Despite adding their infancy narratives of Jesus' birth, both Matthew and Luke retained Mark's adoption formula at the baptism and transfiguration of Jesus. However, because these two Gospel writers have shifted their explanation of Jesus' divine sonship to his birth, God's identification of Jesus as a beloved and chosen son (Mt 3:17; 17:5; Lk 3:22; 9:35) no longer functions as an adoption formula but as a public avowal of the divine paternity.

Jesus the Divine Son Sent from Heaven

More than any other Gospel writer, John stressed the divine sonship of Jesus. John moved beyond natural generation to claim the preexistence of the divine Word (Greek, *logos*, "thought, word, or idea"), who subsequently became flesh as Jesus of Nazareth. John pushed the divine sonship claim back to the time before Jesus' birth: he was a divine being, with God at creation, who was sent into the world to save us from sin and bring us into the right relationship with God.

Thus John's understanding of Jesus' preexistent divine sonship makes his Gospel very different from the other three. John has no need for an adoption formula, so Jesus' baptism was not an occasion for the divine recognition of Jesus' sonship but for the human recognition by John the Baptist and his disciples.

John also had no need for a story of Jesus' birth because Jesus' presence was understood as the incarnation of the divine being in human flesh, the perfect revelation of God to humanity. Thus John was free to use the relational concepts of father/son in new ways to accentuate both Jesus' equality with the Father as divine and his subordination to the Father as Son.

John's special emphasis on the identity of Jesus can be summarized in his oft-repeated idea that Jesus was God's Son sent for salvation. John stressed in an unprecedented way (more than thirty times) that Jesus was sent from God (see for example Jn 4:34 and 10:36). As Son, Jesus was under the authority of the Father and was recognized as sent into the world for judgment and salvation. This mission was closely linked with his divine status as Son of God.

John's use of the sender/sent, father/son categories is his unique contribution to our understanding of Jesus.

Because ancient societies lacked any means of rapid travel or instant communication, messengers were often dispatched as agents to conduct diplomacy, business, and family matters. The Jews recognized that God also sent messengers to carry out God's business on earth. They recognized both angelic messengers (such as Raphael in the book of Tobit or Gabriel in Luke 1:26) and human messengers, such as the prophets (Is 6:8; Jer 1:7).

Jesus as God's Messenger

Whenever a messenger was sent in the ancient world, a general set of guidelines constituted what we might call today a job description that outlined the messenger's powers and directed his behavior. John applied the commonly accepted role of a messenger to express his key ideas about Jesus as

God's messenger. While this application has echoes in the other three Gospels, which also indicate that Jesus was "sent" (Mt 10:40; Mk 9:37; Lk 4:43; 9:48; 10:16), John uses it as the backbone for his distinctive portrait of Jesus as God's Son sent for salvation.

Jesus Is God's Messenger from Heaven

A messenger was necessary when great distance or special circumstance required that the problem be dealt with in an indirect way. As the preexistent, divine Logos, Jesus was God's agent for creation. He was also sent into the world directly from God. Jesus can tell us about God because he has come down from God (Jn 3:13; 6:38; 8:42), and so he alone has experiential knowledge of divine things (Jn 3:12).

Jesus Is Equal to the Father Who Sent Him

A messenger was to be regarded as the sender in the performance of the mission by those with whom he had to deal. Not only does the prologue of John's Gospel affirm the divinity of the Logos as incarnate in Jesus, but Jesus makes the bold claim in 10:30 that "the Father and I are one." Jesus' opponents found this claim extremely problematic (Jn 5:18; 10:33). But as God's unique messenger, to encounter Jesus was to "see the Father" (Jn 14:9; see also 8:19, 29; 10:37–38; 12:44–45; 14:11). Although the ramifications of being equal to God are not spelled out in John's Gospel in detail, they later become the focus for many of the theological debates concerning Christ that raged in the church from the fourth to the sixth centuries.

Jesus Is Commissioned by God to Perform Specific Tasks

A messenger's authority was only for the performance of a specific task or tasks, and the messenger had to obey the sender's instructions. Jesus clearly has come to carry out the mission of God, normally summarized as "salvation." Certainly the most familiar summary of this is John 3:16. "For God so loved the world that he gave his only Son, so that everyone who believes in him may not perish but may have eternal life."

As to Jesus of Nazareth, I think His system of morals and His religion, as He left them to us, the best the world ever saw or is like to see; but I apprehend it has received various corrupting changes, and I have, with most of the present dissenters in England, some doubts as to His divinity.

—*BENJAMIN FRANKLIN*
(1706–1790), American statesman and inventor

Jesus brings salvation not merely by being enfleshed (Jn 1:14) but also by doing the works of God—which include giving life and making judgment (Jn 5:21–22; 9:39), delivering God's message (see, for example, Jn 3:34), glorifying God through prayer and action (see, for example, Jn 2:11; 7:18), and taking care of all those entrusted to him (see, for example, Jn 17:9–19).

Jesus Is Given Full Authority to Complete His Mission

The sender granted the messenger full rights of representation, even to appear in court in the sender's stead. Jesus has been granted the power by God to overcome the hostility of the Jews and of the world because they refused to accept him (Jn 1:10–11). Jesus shares in the power of God (Jn 3:35) to give life and to judge (Jn 5:22, 26–27; 8:16).

Jesus Reports to and Returns to the Father

The messenger had to return and report to the sender and turn over whatever property was involved. Normally, a report would be given to the sender upon the return of the messenger. John artfully changes the sequence by anticipating this future event in the Last Supper discourse of Jesus. The so-called High Priestly Prayer found in John 17 seems more like Jesus' report to the Father on the completion of his mission, together with a prayer that the mission will be continued by the community of disciples after his death.

Jesus also alluded several times to his return to the Father (Jn 12:23; 13:1; 14:28; 17:11). The Christian theological understanding of death as a return home to God is rooted in this Johannine perspective. Jesus' dying words on the cross, "It is finished" (Jn 19:30), also reflect his control over events to the extent that he does not die until his mission is fully accomplished.

Jesus Always Remains Subordinate to the Father

The messenger, while equal to the sender in the performance of the mission, was always subordinate to the sender. Despite Jesus' divine status that renders him almost superhuman in relation to us, John insisted that Jesus was subordinate to the Father. The use of the father/son categories in their first-century context would have implied an understanding of subordination of the Son to the Father.

That Jesus was divine yet not the Father presents in concise form the mystery that would fester among the Jews (If Jesus was of divine status, then why not two Gods?) and confound generations of Christian theologians. John, of course, was not interested in the conceptual explanations of how Jesus can be both equal and yet subordinate to God. He simply presented the concrete descriptions using the father/son terminology.

But Jesus' subordination is explicit when he claims that "I can do nothing on my own" (Jn 5:30; 8:28; 14:16, 28, 31) and "servants are not greater than their master, nor are messengers greater than the one who sent them" (Jn 13:16). Jesus' fidelity to God and obedience as a Son demands that he accept his subordinate place and role in relation to the Father.

The Chain of Messengers

John is not content to apply this messenger model simply to Jesus, but extends it because Jesus also becomes a sender. John recognized that the Christian life was caught up in a network, or chain, of messengers. The Father sent Jesus and the Holy Spirit, whom John calls the Advocate or Paraclete.

Jesus in turn sent the Advocate (Jn 14:26; 15:26; 16:7) and the disciples (Jn 17:8; 20:21) to continue his mission for the forgiveness of sins (salvation). But the fundamental laws of the messenger remain intact in every link of this chain. Although the goals are shared and power to perform the mission is granted, nevertheless a subordination always remains between the sender and messenger.

Through faith in Jesus and personal contact with the Holy Spirit, the Christian community continues the mission and ministry of Jesus. But what was his mission? What were his goals? What tasks did he take as his own? And how did he carry out these tasks? We'll explore these questions in the chapters to come.

PART TWO

What Can You Do?

(John 6:30, NAB)

What is this? A new teaching—with authority!

—*MARK 1:27*

CHAPTER SEVEN

Jesus' Goal: Building God's Kingdom

We can now move from an understanding of Jesus' identity and character to an examination of what he was about. What kinds of deeds are appropriate or expected of a son of honorable character like Jesus? How did he understand the goal of his work for God?

Jesus the Good Son

As an honorable son, Jesus would be expected to be obedient to his father, zealous for the family honor, and eager to help with his father's business. In fact, the Gospels portray his ministry and mission in these exact terms.

Matthew, especially, dwells on Jesus' obedience in relation to God, noting how what Jesus said and did conformed to the fulfillment of so many things that God wanted. Jesus' suffering and death are depicted as the supreme instances of his obedience. Despite his own fears and possible hesitancy, Jesus chose to do not his own will but God's will, as any good son would.

Jesus is also depicted as zealous for his family's honor. Jesus sacrificed the lesser honor of his earthly family for the honor of being the Jewish Messiah. He gave up the honor of being the Jewish Messiah for his role as the Son of man, God's agent for ushering in the kingdom of God. Finally, he dedicated himself totally to the honor associated with being the personal revelation of God the Father as the unique Son of God.

As God's messianic agent in the service of right relationships, Jesus displayed a total dedication to his Father's concerns. He presented the ideal of a just community, using the image of the kingdom of God. The kingdom of God described God's presence in our world and invited persons to create a community that would live in this world according to God's will—in right relationships, based on love and attaining peace for all.

As the Jewish Scriptures make clear, this community of persons in right relationship with God and with one another is the reason God created humanity and came down to restore the relationship broken by humans. God wants this relationship with humans so much that God continually breaks into our world to establish, maintain, and enhance this relationship.

Building God's Kingdom

Have you ever wondered what motivated Jesus to get out of bed every morning? It seems strange to imagine that he awoke, washed his face, put on his tunic, and told himself that he had better get moving on saving the world. But if we carefully analyze the descriptions of Jesus' public life, we notice that he spent his days traversing the Galilean region, teaching about God's kingdom, demonstrating its reality through his healing, and celebrating it through shared meals.

But most important, he invited disciples to follow him and to create a kingdom community in which people would live as if the kingdom of God were the primary reality for their lives. We can sum up Jesus' public ministry by saying that he proclaimed a new way for people to relate to God and to one another. Then he put this vision into practice by building this ideal community with his disciples. This experiment in kingdom living was the goal that kept Jesus busy day after day.

God's Dream for a Kingdom Community

Great human visionaries have dreamed dreams that have changed our world. Jesus understood that God has a dream too. As creator of the universe, God is the original, imaginative dreamer. God's dream of a world was turned into reality at the moment of creation.

> Caesar hoped to reform men by changing institutions and laws;
> Christ wished to remake institutions, and lessen laws, by changing
> men.
>
> —*WILL DURANT*
> historian, *Caesar and Christ*

Although God's original dream was distorted by the evils created by our human decisions and imagination, God continued to dream of new creation transformed by the divine imagination. God's dream for our world continues every day as God sustains the universe in its existence and transforms the flawed original creation.

The story of God's dream is recounted for us in the Bible. God breaks into our world, into our everyday lives, to be present for a relationship. God always appears to us in and through the realities of our familiar world. God searches out individuals who are part of communities—members of families, clans, tribes, and nations—so that those people might create a community that will live according to God's vision. As a result, God's community will always be distinct from human communities.

If we take a quick overview of the Bible, we can see that God's dream for a new community is recounted in the stories of four different communities. Each of these four versions reveals the same general pattern of God's search for a community in which God would hold dominion, where justice would regulate human relationships based on love, and peace (*shalom* in Hebrew, meaning "the fullness of life") would result for all.

God's dream is illustrated in the stories of the Eden community of Adam and Eve (who represent all humanity) told in Genesis 1–11, the *shalom* community of Israel related in Genesis 12 to the end of the Old Testament, the kingdom community of Jesus reported in the Gospels, and the discipleship community of Christians recounted in Luke's book of the Acts of the Apostles.

God as Our Heavenly King

As a Jew, Jesus grew up in the *shalom* community of Israel. For over a millennium, the Jews had been trying to realize God's dream of a community that would contrast with every type of human community. As sons and daughters of Abraham, the Jews understood themselves as not only the family of Abraham but also the family of God.

It is no wonder, then, that Jesus would imagine the ideal community for his disciples as God's family and its members as God's children. Thus Jesus gravitates in his language to the image of God as the heavenly head of the household, who was called upon to protect and provide for all who belonged to the household.

But Jesus also recognized a concept that had all too often been missed, especially in the previous five centuries since the time of the Babylonian exile. In direct contrast to the Jewish attitude that their community should be characterized by a separatist and often elitist attitude as *the* chosen people, Jesus taught that the family of God included all humanity.

Jesus shared God's vision of a new creation, a kingdom in which God's name would be praised and God's will would be done, where reconciliation and forgiveness, service, and the sharing of bread and wine would characterize a community gathered from all peoples, economic ranks, and social strata. Jesus' kingdom community was open to all, regardless of social status, gender, wealth, or religious heritage. God reigned over this community as would a benevolent king. And members of that community must live in right relationships to God and to each other.

Relating to God: Helps from the Patronage Mentality

Whether we are aware of it or not, we are involved in a relationship with God—the mysterious Other. God transcends our reality, yet freely breaks into it to transform it into a reality ordered and guided by our relation to God. Jesus comes "to fulfill all righteousness" (Mt 3:15), that is, to establish and model for us right relationships to God and to others. But how would first-century persons know how to relate to God? What guidelines did they have for relationships of any kind?

In the first-century world, relationships between equals were guided by the protocols of friendship. Relationships between unequals were guided by the practices of patronage. If we understand what patronage was and how it worked, we will appreciate how Jesus understood and explained our relationship to God.

Matthew's gospel says that Jesus was admired because "he was teaching with power." . . . To "teach with power" means he had the power to penetrate the heart.

—THOMAS AQUINAS
(1225–1274), theologian and doctor of the Church, *Commentary on Matthew*

First-century Mediterranean society was characterized by rigidly stratified social classes and a rather weak central authority (law) in which the wealthy, powerful, and well-born controlled access to most of the things necessary to secure a better life.

Those primarily in control of these important resources were not government officials but the heads of families, or patrons. Those who needed these essential resources were called clients (*cliens* in Latin, meaning "to depend on") because acquiring these necessary goods depended upon the relationship with the patron. This system of relationships intensified the importance of personal loyalties rather than law as the cement that held the culture together.

The patronage relationship structured the family. The father's power, authority, and control over the lives of everyone in the extended household (wife, children, slaves) were practically absolute and unchallenged. This pattern of patronal domination was then used to guide other social relationships between unequals (kings to subjects, business patrons to clients, masters to slaves, men to women, adults to children).

Characteristics of Patronage Relationships

Patron-client relationships are

- between unequals in power, wealth, status, learning, etc. (in contrast to friendship, which is a relationship between equals)
- based on open-ended reciprocity, or exchange, in which both parties get what they need
- voluntary (not a legal obligation or "owed" to anyone)
- particular (favoritism is expected!)
- binding on both parties (with social rather than legal sanctions if the obligations are not satisfactorily met)

Because patron-client relationships were not legal contracts, they could not be demanded or required. The patron was under no obligation to give any of his valuable resources to any particular client. Favoritism was at the root of the whole patronage system. The patron always distributed his resources expecting something in return. There was never any notion of a free gift. The client was expected to pay back the favor, not necessarily in kind, as legal contracts might stipulate (for example, paying back a pound of seed with a pound of seed from the next harvest), but with demonstrations of loyalty, praises of honor, and always, expressions of gratitude.

Recall that honor was a central cultural value. This is very different from today's Western culture in which money is the highest value and can be used to acquire honor, status, or privilege. In Jesus' world, honor could be used to generate wealth through the "old boys" network of the well-born and privileged, but wealth could not buy honor or social standing.

How Patronage Works

Patrons (who control goods and resources for securing a better life) initiate the relationship by responding to the requests of clients for help. The patron's side of the relationship involves three dimensions: bestowing favors (benefits, gifts, "graces"), providing what clients need for a better life, and protecting clients from enemies, dangers, and difficult situations. Patrons are characterized by their generosity in providing for and protecting their clients.

Clients (who need goods and resources for survival and sustenance) express their side of the relationship through their response to the patron's generous favors. Their obligations included unquestioned (and unquestioning) loyalty, submission, obedience, and exclusive commitment to the patron. Moreover, public signs and expressions of honor, praise, respect, gratitude, thanks, and a willingness to do other favors when the patron asks are recognized as part of their ongoing responsibility.

God as Patron

In this patronage culture, people applied to their relationship with God (the most powerful patron of all) what was required of them as subordinated clients in other relationships. Their relationship with God was also illustrated both in their use of patron titles (calling God Father, Benefactor, Savior, Lord, Master, and King) and in their description of God's benefits as favors, grace, and mercy.

When God acted toward us out of mercy (just as the patron could freely choose his clients and give them favors and protection), God was acting as a benefactor and a savior. When God acted out of justice, God took the role of judge. Because God was both a patron and a judge, as clients people would pray that the special relationship they had with God, their patron, would influence God's strictness as their judge. They couldn't expect less than justice from God the judge, but they always hoped for patronal favoritism!

A more familiar Christian term that describes God's relationship to us is *grace*. The primary experience of grace, of course, is the gift of God's own self in the covenant relationship. This is the grace that makes us holy (sanctifying grace). God also gives us many other spiritual gifts, which Paul called *charisms,* that we are to use to build up the community (1 Cor 12:1–31).

In today's world, especially in cultures that have grown away from a patriarchal worldview, it seems foreign to think of God as a patron and of ourselves as clients. But our relationship with God is still based upon similar expectations. We look to a God who is beyond our human limitations, whose supreme power and love protect and provide for us. Our part of the relationship is to trust God's benevolence, depend on God's love and help, and give thanks for the gifts God bestows upon us.

How Patronage Has Shaped Christian Prayer

Given the dynamics of a patronage-oriented society, it's not difficult to see the origins of Christian prayer and much of the vocabulary that describes it. God takes the initiative to come down from heaven to be present for a relationship with us. This relationship entails a mutual commitment, a covenant, in which God commits himself to us as our benefactor, provider, and protector.

> Alexander, Caesar, Charlemagne, and I have founded empires. But on what did we rest the creations of our genius? Upon force. Jesus Christ founded his empire upon love; and at this hour millions of men would die for him.
>
> —*NAPOLEON I*
> (1769–1821), French statesman

We, in turn, commit our exclusive loyalty, obedience, and submission to God. But a covenant not only entails commitment to the other person; it is the covenant relationship itself that establishes a community. Thus the covenant partners commit themselves to building and enriching the community created by their mutual commitment.

The two basic types of scriptural prayer—lament and hymn—found in the Psalms are rooted in the behavior of clients toward God the patron. The clients express their dependence and need in cries for help (prayer as lament) and petitions to God. They remind God of God's covenant obligations to bestow favors, provide for their needs, and protect them from harm.

God hears, answers, helps, saves, delivers, rescues, and gives the gift of salvation. The Psalms offer constant evidence of how the heavenly Patron provides for our needs and protects us from enemies. The proper response to this kind of treatment from God includes praise (prayer as hymn), thanks, loyalty, confidence, penitence, intercession, and promises to act more responsibly.

WHAT CAN YOU DO?

The Lord's Prayer

The prayer that Jesus taught his disciples, and which Christians call the Lord's Prayer or the Our Father from its opening words, is also characterized by the reciprocal relationship and obligations of patron and client. The first set of petitions identify God's obligations to us as patron, while the second set express our obligations as clients.

Although we might find it difficult in our contemporary Western culture to think of ourselves as clients and God as patron, giving and receiving are still the foundation of our relationship with God and with one another. We can easily translate mutual responsibility to life as we know it. We learn in any relationship that one person alone cannot make that relationship satisfying or rich. And we learn, often as children, that we are actually in control of very little about our lives. Because we are dependent upon God for our life and for our continued existence, Jesus' prayer teaches us to seek God first for our daily needs and for protection. Our attitudes of praise, thanks, petition, and adoration remain the hallmarks of genuine prayer and of our relationship with God.

Whether you lived in the first century and thought of yourself as a client to God the patron or you are living in this new millennium and think of yourself as someone who is growing in friendship with God, the amazing truth is that God allows us access to the mystery of God's person and that God, who created the universe, is concerned with us as

JESUS' GOAL: BUILDING GOD'S KINGDOM

A PATRONAGE EXPLANATION OF
THE OUR FATHER PRAYER (MATTHEW 6:9–13)

Clients first fulfill their duties,

- calling upon God as their divine patron,
  Our Father in heaven,

- returning praise of God's person,
  hallowed be your name.

- aligning themselves with God's purpose,
  Your kingdom come.

- affirming their obedience to the patron's authority,
  Your will be done,

- desiring to obey completely and perfectly.
  on earth as it is in heaven.

Then they make known their needs,

- requesting that the patron provide what they need,
  Give us this day our daily bread.

- requesting that the patron be lenient in demanding return,
  And forgive us our debts,

- conditioning the patron's action on their own,
  as we also have forgiven our debtors.

- requesting that the patron protect them from difficulties,
  And do not bring us to the time of trial,

- requesting that the patron protect them from their enemies.
  but rescue us from the evil one.

WHAT CAN YOU DO?

individuals, families, communities, and nations. When Jesus called God Father, he sought to bring God closer to us in our own thinking. And because God is understood as a Father, we all become brothers and sisters to one another in the kingdom community that God desires.

Jesus the Teacher of the New Kingdom Way

Jesus was the rabbi, the teacher of the kingdom way of seeing the world and of being in it. This kingdom was focused on God's presence in our world, transforming it from a place marred and disordered by Satan and the powers of evil to a world characterized by the lordship of God and the powers of good. Eradicating evil and transforming all creation into the service of God was the goal of Jesus the Christ. After his death this became the goal of the kingdom community.

Jesus was the teacher of the kingdom, the proclaimer and builder of God's kingdom community. In his very first discourse about the kingdom way of living, recorded in Matthew's Gospel and known as the Sermon on the Mount (Mt 5–7), Jesus spelled out for his would-be disciples his dream of a new community.

Jesus identified the benefits bestowed by God as the Beatitudes, or blessings, that those in the community would share (Mt 5:1–12). He dreamed of a kingdom community in which the poor and oppressed would be blessed, those who mourn would be comforted, and the meek would inherit the land.

He yearned for a kingdom community in which those who hunger and thirst for justice would be satisfied, where the merciful would be shown mercy, and the clean of heart would see God. In his kingdom community, peacemakers would be called God's children, and those persecuted for justice' sake and slandered and treated evilly would find their reward. Jesus' goal was to make this kingdom dream a reality.

Learning from Jesus: Creating the Kingdom Community Today

Anyone who chooses to make a faith commitment to follow Jesus as a Christian is invited to continue the work of Jesus to make this dream of a kingdom community into a reality, to realize the dream by living the kingdom way *now*.

This Christian community will incorporate God's ideas for a radically different type of social existence that so far has not been achieved. To recognize the qualities of this new community, we must use the Bible's stories, examples, instruction, wisdom, and information to realize the dream of God for a community of nondomination, nonviolence, and peaceful conflict resolution. To live this way ensures that Jesus' goal of building God's kingdom on earth will be accomplished.

JESUS IMAGINES THE KINGDOM OF GOD
(MATTHEW 13:44–52)

The kingdom of heaven is like treasure hidden in a field, which someone found and hid; then in his joy he goes and sells all that he has and buys that field.

Again, the kingdom of heaven is like a merchant in search of fine pearls; on finding one pearl of great value, he went and sold all that he had and bought it.

Again, the kingdom of heaven is like a net that was thrown into the sea and caught fish of every kind; when it was full, they drew it ashore, sat down, and put the good into baskets but threw out the bad. So it will be at the end of the age. The angels will come out and separate the evil from the righteous and throw them into the furnace of fire, where there will be weeping and gnashing of teeth.

"Have you understood all this?" They answered, "Yes." And he said to them, "Therefore every scribe who has been trained for the kingdom of heaven is like the master of a household who brings out of his treasure what is new and what is old."

Why do you speak to them in parables?

—*MATTHEW 13:10*

CHAPTER EIGHT

Jesus the Prophet: Disclosing God's Presence

Jesus was no pie-in-the-sky visionary but demonstrated a keen awareness of the practical tasks that had to be completed to bring the kingdom of God into being on earth.

Through the teacher, Christians can see what they literally cannot see: Jesus in the hungry, the thirsty, the strange, the naked, the sick, the imprisoned.

—MARIANNE SAWICKI
theologian, *Seeing the Lord*

At the center of Jesus' kingdom mentality was the conviction that God is in our midst and wants to have a vital relationship with us. Jesus took on more than one role to help people understand this. As a teacher of God's kingdom way he took on roles that were familiar in that place and time: prophet, priest, and king. His mission was to teach us how to discover and celebrate God's presence and to reorder our lives around our experience of God's presence.

Who Were the Prophets, and What Did They Do?

The classic Jewish prophets appeared and flourished in the nation's history at the same time as the kings. In earlier times, Moses exemplified the role of the prophet so that it could be claimed that "never since has there arisen a prophet in Israel like Moses, whom the LORD knew face to face. He was unequaled for all the signs and wonders that the LORD sent him to perform in the land of Egypt, against Pharaoh and all his servants and his entire land, and for all the mighty deeds and all the terrifying displays of power that Moses performed in the sight of all Israel" (Dt 34:10–12).

Moses was not only the leader of the people but also the mediator who heard God's words and communicated them to the people. Prophecy meant to speak on behalf of another, as a messenger would do. He alerted the people to God's presence, clarified what God expected in the covenant relationship, and encouraged the people to heed the words of God's commandments.

As time passed, the people adopted a royal administration for the community. As the early tribal confederation that had characterized the Jewish people since the Exodus gave way to a national state ruled by a king, the prophetic office also evolved.

The king ruled on earth in God's place and in accordance with God's laws. However, the power of kings tempted them to forsake God's ways and to adopt human ways of governing the people. Instead of trusting God and following God's instructions, the kings tended to trust themselves and use their own ideas about how to manage the kingdom.

Especially in times of crisis, neglecting the presence and directives of God was a choice that brought God's judgment on the people. The prophets reminded kings that God was present and active in the political and social circumstances of the community. Like lobbyists for the rule of God, they demanded that the kings' policies and actions follow what God desired and not simply what was most expedient according to human political wisdom.

Their major task was not so much to foretell the future as to reveal God's presence in the events affecting their nation. Prophets like Isaiah and Jeremiah guided the king's behavior when threats from Assyria and Babylonia precipitated decisions (often concerning alliances) that would determine the fate of the nation.

The prophets were especially sensitive to God's presence in the events of national life. Because they were steeped in the traditions of God's word, they gave guidance for action in accordance with these divine commands. They reminded the kings that human analyses of situations and human solutions were never fully adequate.

Political and social situations demanded that the people recognize God's holy presence. Consequently, they must become aware that human evil would provoke God's anger, invite God's punishment of the wicked, and result in God's rescue of the oppressed. So the prophetic task concentrated on the recognition and rooting out of sin, lest God be forced to judge and punish.

The prophets detected certain patterns of God's activity in our world. They recognized that God's presence always created a situation in which first came judgment and then salvation. When God appeared at the time of the Exodus, for example, God's presence meant judgment for their Egyptian oppressors and salvation for the Jewish slaves in Egypt.

God's judgment of sin and reward of salvation were accomplished in and through the political and social life of the people. The prophets recognized that the people's behavior was the most crucial factor. If they sinned, God's judgment would inevitably follow. So the prophet's task was to recognize and proclaim how God was active in the current political, social, and religious situation.

Prophets were familiar with God's past actions, and these became a storehouse of images and patterns for understanding the present. They were also aware of the promise that God's presence would transform everything into something new. So they were extremely sensitive to the extraordinary presence of God in the ordinary events of life. Their evaluations were not merely human but included a divinely inspired perspective that kings and others did not seem to share—or care much about. Through their double vision of the world from both the divine and human viewpoints, prophets taught how to see, evaluate, and act in the world as God instructed.

Prophets encouraged people to hear and heed God's message. They were never just interested in good ideas, but in good lives that met the demands of the right relationships with God and with others. They offered a new vision of the world and demanded that people change themselves and their ways because of God's presence.

How Was Jesus a Prophet?

Jesus was a prophet in many ways. He was steeped in the Scriptures and knew God's laws. He could recognize God's presence in the world, and he could see what the results would be if people continued in their present attitudes and actions. His words were often warnings that people must change their lives and turn to God. Jesus gave people opportunities to judge themselves and change their ways so that God would not have to discipline them.

Jesus knew that God was present in our world. But God, by nature, was not of our world. God was the creator who fashioned everything, but God transcended creation. God was not visible, tangible, or in any way directly accessible to the senses.

But Jesus' vision went further than that of the former prophets. He knew that not only was God present in the world but that "the kingdom of God is at hand." Furthermore, in the person of Jesus, God was present in a way God had never before been present. Jesus' challenge was to reveal God to people not only through extraordinary divine interventions but also through the experiences of ordinary life and work.

The whole Jewish tradition was based on the community's experience of this transcendent God's breaking into the world to relate to them through the voices of the prophets and through miraculous happenings. In his role as prophet, Jesus had to get people to notice something that was beyond their powers of sense perception but not beyond their experience. How could he provide people with eyes to see and ears to hear what normally went unseen and unheard? His answer was to use the stories that we call parables.

One of the most helpful descriptions of a parable was given by the British Scripture scholar C. H. Dodd. "At its simplest the parable is a metaphor or simile drawn from nature or common life, arresting the hearer by its vividness or strangeness and leaving the mind in sufficient doubt about its precise application to tease it into active thought" (*The Parables of the Kingdom,* p. 5).

JESUS' PARABLES

Parable	Mark	Matthew	Luke
the doorkeeper	13:33–37	___	___
the faithful servant	___	24:45–51	12:42–46
the fig tree	13:28–29	24:32–33	21:29–31
the friend at midnight	___	___	11:5–8
the good Samaritan	___	___	10:29–37
the great supper	___	22:1–14	14:16–24
the hidden treasure	___	13:44	___
the laborers in the vineyard	___	20:1–16	___
the leaven	___	13:33	13:20–21
the lost coin	___	___	15:8–10
the lost sheep	___	18:12–14	15:4–7
the lost son	___	___	15:11–32
the mustard seed	4:30–32	13:31–32	13:18–19
the net	___	13:47–50	___
the pearl	___	13:45–46	___
the Pharisee and the tax collector	___	___	18:9–14
the rich fool	___	___	12:13–21
the rich man and Lazarus	___	___	16:19–31
the seed growing secretly	4:26–29	___	___
the sheep and the goats	___	25:31–46	___
the sower and the soils	4:3–9	13:3–9	8:5–8
the talents	___	25:14–30	19:11–27
the ten maidens	___	25:1–13	___
the two debtors	___	___	7:41–43
the two sons	___	21:28–32	___
the unjust steward	___	___	16:1–8
the unmerciful servant	___	18:23–35	___
the wheat and the weeds	___	13:24–30	___
the wicked tenants	12:1–11	21:33–45	20:9–18
the widow and the judge	___	___	18:1–8

Jesus' parables were apparently innocent stories or analogies that forced the audience to change the way they thought about their world. When Jesus spoke in parables, he invited his audience to use their imaginations to enter a world that saw things from God's point of view.

In some cases, Jesus' message was so hard-hitting, so confrontational, that almost of necessity it had to be wrapped in the layered skins of parable. Teased by parable into ongoing reflection, his audience could be invited into an interpretive dance leading them from the comfort of the status quo to self-criticism to personal and social transformation.

—*JOEL B. GREEN*
Scripture scholar, *The Theology of the Gospel of Luke*

The parables are Jesus' teaching tool through which we can learn how to discover the deeper meaning of the reality we live in. Jesus reminds us that the bedrock foundation of our existence is that we are related to God. Although transcendent and invisible, God comes into our experience in order to relate to us.

Jesus' parables are his way of teaching people a new way of seeing the world and then being in it. They move people beyond the conventional view that God is absent or too distant from our world to make a difference. In this world, other powers, not God, rule our everyday lives. But Jesus' parables summon us to a new view. What if God were present for a relationship with us? What if God were King and effectively ruled our world? What then?

WHAT CAN YOU DO?

Jesus' parables teach us how to observe the ordinary happenings of our lives to discover that some very extraordinary things are going on. The parables open up a world beyond the limits of our normal perception where even our most ordinary everyday activities are charged with the presence of God. They offer us a way to imagine and understand how God works in everyday events. When we learn to notice this extraordinary transformative power of God lurking beyond the margins of our normal perceptions, then we begin to see things in a new way and notice things that we never did before. As people of faith who believe that there is more to reality than meets the eye, we need to develop skills for discovering this hidden dimension of our lives.

Jesus Christ belonged to the true race of prophets. He saw with open eye the mystery of the soul.

—*RALPH WALDO EMERSON*
(1803–1882), American philosopher and essayist

How Do We Relate Jesus' Parables to Life Today?

In order to decipher the meaning of a parable, we must remember that a parable is symbolic speech. Like a code, it always refers to something other than itself. As a kind of symbolic code, a parable joins the world of the story and the world of its audience. Jesus' parables encoded the world in

JESUS THE PROPHET: DISCLOSING GOD'S PRESENCE

which God was king. Jesus' stories of masters and servants, farmers, and household members are not self-contained but point to the surprising ways that God relates to us and expects us to relate to God and to one another.

When we read a parable (see page 125 for a list of Jesus' parables), we need to make a connection between the people and events in the parable and the people and events of our own lives. The Gospel writers themselves suggest how to relate different types of ground (parable of the sower) to the ministry of Jesus (see Mk 4:13–20; Mt 13:18–23; Lk 8:11–15). Another example is Matthew's application of the parable of the wheat and the weeds that grow side by side from the seeds planted in persons by Jesus and the devil. Only the final harvest will make clear who are the wheat and who are the weeds (Mt 13:36–43).

As you might have guessed, how people understand and apply parables is always open-ended. For two millennia, Jesus' parables have been constantly interpreted and reinterpreted because the historical, social, and cultural situations of the audience changed over time.

But the main points of the parables—God's presence and how we can relate to God and to one another—have remained permanently applicable. These stories given to us by Jesus reveal some of God's favorite patterns of relating.

JESUS' PARABLE OF THE GOOD SAMARITAN
(LUKE 10:25–37)

Just then a lawyer stood up to test Jesus. "Teacher," he said, "what must I do to inherit eternal life?" He said to him, "What is written in the law? What do you read there?" He answered, "You shall love the Lord your God with all your heart, and with all your soul, and with all your strength, and with all your mind; and your neighbor as yourself." And he said to him, "You have given the right answer; do this, and you will live."

But wanting to justify himself, he asked Jesus, "And who is my neighbor?" Jesus replied, "A man was going down from Jerusalem to Jericho, and fell into the hands of robbers, who stripped him, beat him, and went away, leaving him half dead. Now by chance a priest was going down that road; and when he saw him, he passed by on the other side. So likewise a Levite, when he came to the place and saw him, passed by on the other side. But a Samaritan while traveling came near him; and when he saw him, he was moved with pity. He went to him and bandaged his wounds, having poured oil and wine on them. Then he put him on his own animal, brought him to an inn, and took care of him. The next day he took out two denarii, gave them to the innkeeper, and said, 'Take care of him; and when I come back, I will repay you whatever more you spend.' Which of these three, do you think, was a neighbor to the man who fell into the hands of the robbers?" He said, "The one who showed him mercy." Jesus said to him, "Go and do likewise."

JESUS THE PROPHET: DISCLOSING GOD'S PRESENCE

Learning from Jesus: To See as Jesus Did

Jesus teaches us to look for God's presence in ordinary life. Things that at first appear merely secular—marriage, family, child rearing, jobs, relations with others in the community, and job transfers and other changes in our life—are not understood simply as "just the way things are" but are seen as bearers of God's own presence. In these events we learn to discover God.

Jesus' way of teaching through parables was such a pastoral act of prophetic imagination in which he invited his community of listeners out beyond the visible realities of Roman law and the ways in which Jewish law had grown restrictive in his time. . . . The stories intend to characterize an alternative society which he calls "kingdom of God" but the stories do not offer blueprints, budgets, or programs. They only tease the listeners to begin to turn loose of the givens of the day and to live toward a new social possibility.

—*WALTER BRUEGGEMANN*
Scripture scholar, *Hopeful Imagination: Prophetic Voices in Exile*

The events of our ordinary life disclose the profound, elusive, and extraordinary presence of God. We can never discount this type of revelation of God by limiting our search for God to the mighty deeds of God long ago. God is always coming to us in our everyday situations, inviting and drawing us into a new situation, pulling together things that we never thought were sacred, and luring us into a deeper relationship. God finds us, where we are, to be with us.

WHAT CAN YOU DO?

When we are able to approach others around us—spouses, children, coworkers, acquaintances—as parables, then our world is changed forever. What if God were present in them? What then? How would our behavior change toward them?

These are the kinds of questions we will face when we begin to read our lives as parables of God's presence. And when we do, we will know exactly what Jesus meant when he said, "The kingdom of God is not coming with things that can be observed; nor will they say, 'Look, here it is!' or 'There it is!' For, in fact, the kingdom of God is among you" (Lk 17:20–21).

JESUS' PARABLE ABOUT THE RESPONSE TO HIS TEACHING (MARK 4:2–9)

He began to teach them many things in parables, and in his teaching he said to them:

"Listen! A sower went out to sow. And as he sowed, some seed fell on the path, and the birds came and ate it up. Other seed fell on rocky ground, where it did not have much soil, and it sprang up quickly, since it had no depth of soil. And when the sun rose, it was scorched; and since it had no root, it withered away. Other seed fell among thorns, and the thorns grew up and choked it, and it yielded no grain. Other seed fell into good soil and brought forth grain, growing up and increasing and yielding thirty and sixty and a hundredfold." And he said, "Let anyone with ears to hear listen!"

JESUS THE PROPHET: DISCLOSING GOD'S PRESENCE

Why do you eat and drink
with tax collectors and sinners?

—*LUKE 5:30*

CHAPTER NINE

Jesus the Priest: Celebrating God's Presence

Jesus was more than just a prophet who taught people to see God's presence in the midst of everyday life. He also invited people to discover ways to enter into communion with God. Jesus' goal of building the kingdom included building relationships between people and God the king.

From time immemorial, humans have used rituals and recitals in story and song to celebrate relationships. When the relationship involves the divine, these recitals and rituals become religious. The very word *religion* (Latin, *re-ligare*, "to tie again") is rooted in the notion of "rebinding" persons in relationships.

Religion is based on an understanding of an original relationship that somehow has broken down—where communication has failed, infidelity has weakened mutual commitment, or unloving actions have destroyed community. Religion is the way that the disordered relationship can be restored to harmony. The traditional role of the priest was to help people maintain their relationship with God.

The Priestly Task: Mediating Communion with God

Priests are mediators between God and the human community. They communicate God's word and will to the people and intercede by presenting the community's needs and prayers to God. Priests thus become specialists in the sacred, caring for God's sanctuary or temple, with all of its holy objects, rituals, and persons. Their concern is to sanctify, or make holy, the people's relationship with God through prayer and sacrifice.

For the Israelites, holiness described what made God different from all creation. Holiness was associated with God's transcendent otherness. Holiness was not something that people could achieve on their own. Rather, it was communicated through contact with God. Thus anything involving this contact with God was considered holy. Places such as the temple, people such as the priests, even objects such as the altar were seen as holy through their contact with God.

In Israel, the priestly work of mediating God's will to the people included interpreting the meaning of the covenant law and speaking divine oracles, especially for the forgiveness of sin. Priestly work on behalf of the people included offering sacrifices to God for the people. Although we equate sacrifice with killing or offering something up, the root meaning of sacrifice is to make something holy.

The dedication to God of animals, crops, or the firstborn son was a way of recognizing God's power to give life. It was fitting to offer that life back to God by a ritual killing of the animal or a burning of the gift. (Israelites were not allowed to offer children as sacrifice, according to the law God had given them.) The completeness of the offering was demonstrated by holding nothing back. Because life was associated with blood, the priest sprinkled the animal's blood on the altar of sacrifice and on the people to remind them that their life was a gift from God and so belonged to God.

The Priestly Task in Israel

From Israel's beginning to the time of Jesus, the priestly functions and roles varied according to the changing social and religious situations. From Abraham to the Exodus, the priestly functions were fulfilled by the head of the family, who offered sacrifice on behalf of the family and interpreted God's will for them.

During the Exodus, Moses combined in himself the roles of prophet, priest, and leader. Designated by God as the mediator, Moses communicated God's law to the people and interceded for the people with God. However, the roles of prophetic leader and priest were quickly separated when Aaron was made priest and Moses remained prophetic leader. This separation of priest from leader and from prophet characterized Judaism until the postexilic period.

Up to this day no one has ever been loved as much as Jesus Christ is loved and in the future likewise no one will ever be loved as much as he is loved.

—*POPE PIUS XI*
Encyclical Letter, Dec. 11, 1925

During the two centuries or so between the Exodus and the inauguration of the united kingdom under King David, priests conducted worship at several sanctuaries. But when Solomon, David's son and successor, built the temple at Jerusalem, worship was centralized under the Jerusalem priesthood.

The construction of Solomon's temple and the unification of worship created a kind of professionalized priesthood. Priests assisted the king through explaining God's law, conducted the daily sacrifices, and took care of the business of running the temple. Because the Jerusalem temple was considered the only place on earth where God dwelt, its rites alone were considered valid. Only the annual Passover meal that recounted the Exodus liberation continued to be celebrated in households rather than in the temple.

WHAT CAN YOU DO?

When this first temple was destroyed in 587 B.C. by the Babylonians and the king and people were sent into exile, the social and religious character of the people was altered. After the Exile, the Jews were subject to the great world powers: Persia, Greece, and Rome. Without a king, priests assumed the leadership role and merged the leader-priest roles that had been separated since the time of Moses.

The result was that the postexilic emphases in Judaism shifted dramatically. Because priests were in charge, the royal agenda of independent nationalism gave way to the holiness agenda. Priestly authority replaced the authority of the king, and holiness meant being set apart for God. The priests believed that only with this dedication to holiness would the people survive and prosper.

Priests and the Holiness Agenda

The first order of business when the Jews returned from their exile in Babylon was to rebuild the temple, which was considered necessary if the people were to commune with God properly. The second temple was begun about 536 B.C. and was initially completed and dedicated in 515 B.C. Although not as impressive as Solomon's temple had been (Ezr 3:12), still it was the sign of God's rule, and it provided once again a direct connection between the people and God. To the

Israelite nation, God's presence in the world was to be found in the temple.

The Jerusalem temple was a microcosm of all creation. As God's earthly dwelling place, the temple was at once a concrete embodiment of the holiness of God and a symbol of the community's connection to that holiness. Because God's holy presence was restricted to the temple, God was accessible only through the mediation of the professional priests and their rituals.

Like a guide to the hill passes, Jesus took short cuts across the untraversable mountains of class pride, intellectual arrogance and professional specialization.

—LEWIS MUMFORD
cultural analyst and scholar, *The Condition of Man*

When the people were no longer in exile and had a temple once again, the next important task was to rebuild their community as a community of God's people. They needed to think seriously about what it meant to be God's covenant people. So the restored community made holiness their primary agenda. They would become a holy people in a holy land worshiping in a holy temple.

This holiness agenda was evident from their focus on the importance of the Torah (God's instruction or law for their way of life), the temple (the connecting point of divine and human reality), and the territory (a holy land consecrated

WHAT CAN YOU DO?

by God's presence and the work of the people to become holy). The people could justify their emphasis on holiness because they believed that holiness was God's most important characteristic. After all, God had said to Moses: "Speak to all the congregation of the people of Israel and say to them: You shall be holy, for I the LORD your God am holy" (Lv 19:2).

With holiness as the focus of community life, certain dynamics were put in place. The people believed that if they were God's chosen people, they must be separate from other peoples (Ezr 9:12). This separatist attitude came to be expressed in an extreme concern for boundaries, rigid classification of what was acceptable ("clean") and unacceptable ("unclean"), and strict obedience to God's law. Consequently, life in this postexilic Jewish community was distinguished by

- separation from non-Jews
- no intermarriage with foreigners (Ezr 10:10–11)
- a strictly enforced Sabbath observance
- emphasis on circumcision as a sign of difference
- careful attention to clean/unclean categories for all of life
- emphasis on kosher food regulations
- careful and complete obedience to the whole Torah (all 613 commands)

It's not hard to imagine how the people could develop these attitudes after years of being in exile and not having a temple, which served not only as a center of worship but also as a center of their identity. Their experience of exile and restoration created a mentality that focused the people much more on their own problems. Just as people suffering pain focus more on themselves for healing, so the Judaic community focused more on itself and on the massive task of restoring itself to health. The result, however, created an inward-directed orientation that lingered for centuries.

Jesus' Priestly Task and the Mercy Agenda

Jesus was not really a priest in the Jewish sense. He was not from the priestly family of Aaron, nor did he function in the temple ceremonies. During his ministry, people did not identify him formally as a priest. (In fact, even within Christianity there was no clear emphasis on his priestly character until the letter to the Hebrews, which is the only developed reflection on Jesus' priestly status and function in the whole New Testament.) But because he performed the priestly task of mediating and celebrating the people's relation to God, he can be considered a priestly figure.

But Jesus offered an alternative vision for life in the covenant community. Instead of God's holiness, Jesus stressed God's mercy. He proclaimed God as king: the heavenly patron, or benefactor, who has mercy and generously gives us what we need. Because of our needs, our lives are at the mercy of God, who alone can satisfy them. From this perspective, Jesus offers an agenda that is based on the mercy of God and expects us to imitate God's mercy in our behavior toward others. This agenda is summarized by Jesus when he tells his audience, "Be merciful, just as your Father is merciful" (Lk 6:36).

Conversion to this new understanding of God was not easy. Despite being with Jesus and hearing his teachings, even Peter didn't seem to get the point about God's mercy and its importance for determining who enters the kingdom. So God revealed to him in a dream that Jesus' kingdom community was open to everyone because "God shows no partiality, but in every nation anyone who fears him and does what is right is acceptable to him" (Acts 10:34–35). This insight changed not only Peter's outlook but also the whole future of the church as it opened its doors to Gentiles.

Jesus emphasized that God is impartial. God cannot be bribed or manipulated. God freely bestows gifts and graces on each and every person as God alone wishes. God's generosity is free, unaffected by our desires and uncontrolled by our rules.

The clash of these two agendas—holiness and mercy—was evident when some Pharisees challenged Jesus' eating with tax collectors and sinners, who were ritually unclean and thus not allowed to enter community worship. Jesus retorted with a challenge of his own. "Those who are well

JESUS' ADVICE ON HOW TO PRAY

The Lord's Prayer (Luke 11:1–4)

He was praying in a certain place, and after he had finished, one of his disciples said to him, "Lord, teach us to pray, as John taught his disciples." He said to them, "When you pray, say:

Father, hallowed be your name.
  Your kingdom come.
  Give us each day our daily bread.
  And forgive us our sins,
    for we ourselves forgive everyone indebted to us.
  And do not bring us to the time of trial."

The Friend at Midnight (Luke 11:5–13)

And he said to them, "Suppose one of you has a friend, and you go to him at midnight and say to him, 'Friend, lend me three loaves of bread; for a friend of mine has arrived, and I have nothing to set before him.' And he answers from within, 'Do not bother me; the door has already been locked, and my children are with me in bed; I cannot get up and give you anything.' I tell you, even though he will not get up and give him anything because he is his friend, at least because of his persistence he will get up and give him whatever he needs.

"So I say to you, Ask, and it will be given you; search, and you will find; knock, and the door will be opened for you. For everyone who asks receives, and everyone who searches finds, and for everyone who knocks, the door will be opened. Is there anyone among you who, if your child asks for a fish, will give a snake instead of a fish? Or if the child asks for an egg, will give a scorpion? If you then, who are evil, know how to give good gifts to your children, how much more will the heavenly Father give the Holy Spirit to those who ask him!"

WHAT CAN YOU DO?

The Unjust Judge (Luke 18:1–8)

Then Jesus told them a parable about their need to pray always and not to lose heart. He said, "In a certain city there was a judge who neither feared God nor had respect for people. In that city there was a widow who kept coming to him and saying, 'Grant me justice against my opponent.' For a while he refused; but later he said to himself, 'Though I have no fear of God and no respect for anyone, yet because this widow keeps bothering me, I will grant her justice, so that she may not wear me out by continually coming.'" And the Lord said, "Listen to what the unjust judge says. And will not God grant justice to his chosen ones who cry to him day and night? Will he delay long in helping them? I tell you, he will quickly grant justice to them. And yet, when the Son of Man comes, will he find faith on earth?"

The Pharisee and the Tax Collector (Luke 18:9–14)

He also told this parable to some who trusted in themselves that they were righteous and regarded others with contempt: "Two men went up to the temple to pray, one a Pharisee and the other a tax collector. The Pharisee, standing by himself, was praying thus, 'God, I thank you that I am not like other people: thieves, rogues, adulterers, or even like this tax collector. I fast twice a week; I give a tenth of all my income.' But the tax collector, standing far off, would not even look up to heaven, but was beating his breast and saying, 'God, be merciful to me, a sinner!' I tell you, this man went down to his home justified rather than the other; for all who exalt themselves will be humbled, but all who humble themselves will be exalted."

have no need of a physician, but those who are sick. Go and learn what this means, 'I desire mercy, not sacrifice.' For I have come to call not the righteous but sinners" (Mt 9:12–13).

Jesus' whole ministry was a commentary on this passage from the prophet Hosea (6:6): "For I desire steadfast love and not sacrifice, the knowledge of God rather than burnt offerings." If mercy or steadfast love, that is, the kind of love that characterizes God's covenant love, was superior to the temple sacrifices, then how much more to the laws of ritual impurity and the regulations for keeping the Sabbath (Mt 12:7)? Jesus' new imperative for those wanting to live according to the mercy agenda was: "Be merciful [compassionate], just as your Father is merciful" (Lk 6:36). This captured the essence of Jesus' proclamation that God was the heavenly Father who bestowed all good gifts on humanity.

Jesus' Priestly Teaching Strategy: The Common Meal

Jesus functioned as a priest not because he offered sacrifice but because he introduced a different way that we have access to God's presence for a relationship. He did this through redefining the community meal.

Jesus offered people a way to God that was not connected to the Jerusalem temple and its rites. Through his parables, Jesus reminded people that God's holy presence consecrated not just the temple but everything—the whole of our life.

Because people had access to God's holy presence in their ordinary lives, they no longer were restricted to the professional priesthood as the sole mediators of their relationship with God. God's presence could happen anywhere, at any time, whenever ordinary life broke open to disclose God's extraordinary presence. The great sign of this equality and unrestricted access to God and God's gifts was the common meal.

We cannot overestimate the importance of how Jesus shared meals with people. His example was the primary means of giving people a new picture of how the kingdom relationship with God and with others was to be celebrated and lived out.

Deciphering a Meal

Whether in family dining rooms, school lunchrooms, or five-star restaurants, the meal reveals much about the social group that shares it.

- It defines group boundaries and reinforces group identity (who is "in" and who is "out").
- It marks differences between groups and within groups. (Do you eat with the boss? the janitor?)

- It involves mutual, reciprocal, and often formally unexpressed obligations to give, receive, and repay. ("Is it our turn to invite them over?")

- It symbolizes human interaction, feelings, and relationships (marking special occasions like birthdays, graduations, and anniversaries).

- It mediates social status and power ("Let's do lunch" to close the deal or to be seen by our competitors).

As we examine Jesus' meals, we begin to grasp his vision of the kingdom of God. Meals are not only about food but also about relationships. Anthropologist Mary Douglas, in her famous essay on "Deciphering a Meal," tells us that "if food is treated as a code, the messages it encodes will be found in the pattern of social relations being expressed. The message is about different degrees of hierarchy, inclusion and exclusion, boundaries and transactions across boundaries. Like sex, the taking of food has a social component, as well as a biological one" (in *Myth, Symbol, and Culture,* ed. Clifford Geertz, p. 61).

What the evangelists say through stories about what Jesus did for people, we also say through ritual action with bread and wine. Both the stories and the rituals are in their own way interpretations of Jesus; they are different ways of saying who he is for us.

—TAD GUZIE
sacramental theologian

Jesus showed us that taking food also has religious overtones because it can reveal that God is present in communion with us through the meal celebration. In the sacred meal ritual, God chooses to be present with us for a relationship that brings salvation. Salvation can be described as God's action through Jesus Christ in the Holy Spirit to put us into communion (the right relationship, or covenant friendship) with God and with others. Our lifelong task is to make sure that we begin, continue, and increase this communion.

Communion with another depends on that person being present to us. But personal presence is not limited to physical presence. Spouses, children, friends, enemies, parents, teachers, mentors, business associates, or any other important people can be present to us through our imagination and memory. They can influence us even though they are thousands of miles away or long dead.

Jesus' Meals: The Kingdom of God Is Here

Because meals are all about relationships, Jesus' meals reveal his idea of right relationships with God and with others. Peter Farb and George Armelagos explain that "in all societies, both simple and complex, eating is the primary way of initiating and maintaining human relationships. . . . Once the anthropologist finds out where, when, and with whom the food is eaten, just about everything else can be inferred about the relations among the society's members. . . . To know what, where, how, when, and with whom people eat is to know the character of their society" (*Consuming Passions: The Anthropology of Eating,* pp. 4, 211).

So when we consider where, how, when, and with whom Jesus eats, we will know what the kingdom of God is like. His actions at meals reveal the community relationships that he encourages and the values that characterize life in the kingdom of God.

More than any other Gospel writer, Luke uses Jesus' meal behavior to reveal what it means for followers of Jesus to be people whose lives are shaped by the Christian ritual meal, or Eucharist (from the Greek word for "thanksgiving"), that they celebrate each week in his memory. Jesus always seems to be on the way to a meal, eating a meal, or talking about the meal as a sign of the blessings God has in store for us when the final age of the world arrives.

Sprinkled throughout Luke's Gospel are ten meals. Eight are eaten with Jesus the "prophet mighty in deed and word" (Lk 24:19) in his ministry. Two others are shared with the risen Christ after the Resurrection. But in every instance, Luke uses Jesus and the others present at the meal to reveal how the kingdom community is to live.

By examining Jesus' meals, we discover the symbolic power of his meal behavior to challenge the accepted social customs of his day and to pave the way for a new style of community living that redefines people and erases the artificial boundaries that separate them.

JESUS' MEALS IN LUKE'S GOSPEL

1. Luke 5:27–39   In the house of Levi, the tax collector
2. Luke 7:36–50   In the house of Simon the Pharisee
3. Luke 9:10–17   In the wilderness near Bethsaida
4. Luke 10:38–42   In the house of Martha and Mary
5. Luke 11:37–54   In the house of a Pharisee
6. Luke 14:1–24   In the house of a Pharisee on a Sabbath
7. Luke 19:1–10   In the house of Zacchaeus
8. Luke 22:14–38   Jesus' last supper with the disciples
9. Luke 24:13–35   With the risen Lord at Emmaus
10. Luke 24:36–53   With the risen Lord at Jerusalem

Jesus' table companions express the diversity of the kingdom. Jesus dines with men and women, friends and foes, rich and poor, Pharisees and priests of the religious establishment, tax collectors and "sinners." *Sinner* was both a specific and a generic term. As specific, it identified a person who had done some public action in violation of the commandments. As generic, it identified persons who were constantly in a state of "impurity" that prevented them from participating in the community rituals. This included sick people, like lepers or those possessed of evil spirits, and those with certain

JESUS THE PRIEST: CELEBRATING GOD'S PRESENCE

occupations, like tax collectors and tanners, whose contact with Gentile belongings and blood kept them almost always in a state of "impurity."

Jesus' inclusiveness cut across all the usual social boundaries of his day. His inclusion of men and women challenged the division of gendered space and the hierarchy of male domination. His inclusion of the poor erased the implicit notion that only the rich are blessed by God or worthy to receive God's blessings. He challenged the Pharisees' and priests' self-righteous attitudes. In fact, his meals erase all the usual distinctions and boundaries that delineated his society.

Jesus' meal behavior summarized what he was trying to teach about the kingdom. Instead of the holiness agenda of a people set apart, he invited people to gather in solidarity and compassion. He shifted the emphasis from the holiness concern for sacrifice to that of shared eating, from the holiness restriction of God's presence on the altar to the unrestricted access of the household table, from the holiness stress on separatism and exclusiveness enforced by strict and rigid boundaries to an inclusiveness that broke down boundaries and fostered a new, holy communion among those with whom he dined.

The kingdom meal not only signified the shift from the holiness to the mercy agenda, but it was also a living symbol of God's character as their heavenly benefactor—the giver of all good things. In response to the awareness of God's presence in their midst, Jesus invited his followers to celebrate a communion meal as a community of compassion.

The sheer gift of this presence transformed their ordinary lives into something extraordinary and evoked the demand for thanksgiving (Greek, *eucharist*). Moreover, this meal was a concrete example of the kind of behavior that kingdom living demanded. Jesus' meal behavior guided their hopes for communion and community.

Jesus' teaching about meals was illustrated most completely in his final supper with his disciples on the night before he died. Because of slightly different chronologies about whether the Passover was on Friday or Saturday in the year Jesus died, this meal is described as a Passover meal by Matthew, Mark, and Luke and a farewell supper by John.

In either case, the most surprising element is Jesus' promise to be present again in the bread and cup of wine whenever the disciples celebrated this meal in his memory. Jesus' meal presence with them continued in a new and different way after his death and resurrection. This reality is the root of the Christian Eucharist celebrated today in Jesus' memory.

Learning from Jesus: To Eat as Jesus Did

As we read the stories of Jesus' meal sharing and find ourselves at meals with Jesus, we discover that the people in these stories represent various aspects of ourselves that are still being challenged today. We learn how we are all invited to live the reality of God's kingdom now. If we want to follow Jesus, then we must learn to see the world as Jesus does, to evaluate it as Jesus does, so that we will act as Jesus does.

Just as the magnificent view of our planet from space shows no human boundaries, so God's perspective disregards the human ways we organize our world. Our evaluations of people based on gender, race, citizenship, wealth, status, and authority are not necessarily God's.

Jesus challenges our human communities to embody this openness and inclusiveness. Like Jesus, we must acquire a view of people that refuses to exclude them or deny them their dignity as children of God and brothers and sisters of Jesus. We must imitate God's impartiality by inviting everyone to belong to Jesus' kingdom community.

By inviting us into communion with himself, Jesus invites us into a lifetime process of maturing in our relationships. The community of Christian believers remembers and makes available communion with God through symbols and rituals called sacraments. A sacrament is a visible sign of the hidden reality of salvation. When the gathered assembly— priest and people—performs these symbolic actions, God's power makes what they represent actually occur.

A ritual is a repeated action that helps us bring to consciousness what is always going on but is seldom noticed.

WHAT CAN YOU DO?

The sacred ritual of the Eucharist—the kingdom meal—reminds us that we must give thanks because we are constantly receiving the gifts of God for salvation and sustenance.

The eucharistic mystery is the ritual expression of this communion of all humanity under God's rule. By celebrating this ritual, we experience God's effective influence over us. Christ's presence in the Christian assembly, in the Scripture we read and hear, in the consecrated bread and cup, and in the person of others invites us to be united with him. Our communion grows through the ritual actions of receiving and giving, gathering to immerse ourselves in God's Word, sharing a sacred meal, and eagerly accepting the commission to carry on Christ's work for the world.

Following the example of Jesus, Christians take, bless, break, and share the bread and cup. But simultaneously through God's mysterious power they are taken, blessed, broken, and shared with others as Jesus was. Their everyday lives become a eucharistic experience. God's new table is all-inclusive and demands a heightened sense of inner readiness. To share the kingdom meal is to be in solidarity with Jesus and his mission to build the kingdom community.

What sign can you do,

that we may see and believe in you?

—*JOHN 6:30, NAB*

CHAPTER TEN

Jesus the King: Reordering Life in God's Presence

Once we discover and celebrate God's presence, we are ready to change our lives because of this relationship. Jesus could not usher in the new kingdom simply by revealing God's presence (through his prophet's role) and celebrating God's presence (through his priestly role). He also had to reorder peoples' lives in light of the God they had encountered and celebrated.

Jesus as King

In the ancient hierarchical society, the king stood at the pinnacle of power and privilege, wealth and authority. He brought order into the chaos of life through his wisdom and power. His constant concern was the welfare of the people.

Kings in Israel assumed the same tasks as kings in other nations but with certain nuances. Designated by God, Jewish kings were anointed at their coronation to rule the covenant people in God's place. Promoting the national agenda and ensuring the welfare of the people required that a king use his wisdom to interpret God's guidelines and to carry out policies that were in harmony with God's law.

He was exactly what the man with a delusion never is: he was wise; he was a good judge.

—*G. K. CHESTERTON*
(1874–1936), British poet and essayist, *The Everlasting Man*

As a re-former of peoples' lives, Jesus took on the role of a king. Through his wisdom he articulated the worldview of God's kingdom. Through his power, he proved God's rule over the world by signs and wonders, which we call miracles.

The Gospel writers recognized that Jesus was of the royal Davidic line (son of David) and hence qualified to be the anointed royal figure—the messiah, or christ, that many were expecting. But Jesus consistently refused to identify his kingly task with direct political action, especially a rebellion against the dominant power of the Roman Empire.

However, Jesus exhibited the royal qualities of wisdom and power. As a wisdom teacher, he outlined the kingdom worldview that would guide his followers. His signs and wonders were evidence of and participated with the divine

WHAT CAN YOU DO?

power that was reordering Jewish covenant life into a new community in which God ruled as king and everyone was equal as brothers and sisters (Mt 23:8–9).

Jesus the Wisdom Teacher

For first-century readers, Jesus would be easily recognized as a wisdom teacher who could communicate insight into the right way to live. His examples, vocabulary, colorful stories, and message were not concerned with the intricacies of the Jewish law that preoccupied the schools of rabbinic debate. He answered legal questions mostly because these were the agenda of the scribes and Pharisees, but his answers displayed a freshness and insight that seemed to perplex the learned.

When Jesus spoke about God's rule, he drew from his own experience of God's presence. Jesus did not simply discuss abstract truths, he expressed profound truths in a way that even the unlearned could appreciate.

Most of Jesus' teaching fit comfortably within the conventional wisdom traditions of Israel. Originally collected to educate the king and his royal courtiers, these teachings offered practical advice on the best way to gain wisdom, to learn from nature, to carry on human relationships, and to resolve conflicts.

JESUS' MOST FAMOUS SERMON
(MATTHEW 5:1–7:29)

Jesus' first lesson for disciples seeking the kingdom is found in his Sermon on the Mount (Matthew, chapters 5–7). In the first of five major discourses that form the backbone of Matthew's Gospel, we learn the basic guidelines of living Jesus' way—the ABCs of discipleship.

Jesus is presented as the authoritative teacher of the new Torah. The narratives of chapters 1–4 portrayed Jesus as a "new Moses." Now Jesus the teacher presents the basic principles for living as Christian disciples in the new kingdom. He reveals what our Christian attitudes, beliefs, and commitments must be in order for us to see the world as he does and so act as he does.

I. Opening

- 5:2–12: The Beatitudes, identifying those whom God blesses and their reward, express the essential spiritual characteristics of a true disciple, who must have the poor person's complete trust in and dependence upon God alone.

- The special character of the disciples is to be salt and light for the world.

II. Body of the Sermon

- 5:17–19: The perfection of Jesus' messianic guidelines is contrasted with the law of Moses. The perfection and the "more" of Jesus' demands are explained in 5:21–48.

- 5:20: The greater response that is expected from Christians is contrasted with the response of the Pharisees. The greater response is elaborated on in 6:1–7:12.

- 5:21–48: Jesus' authority is contrasted with that of Moses, and Jesus' guidelines are explained as the completion and perfection of Moses' law.
- 6:1–7:12: The way of true (Christian) discipleship is contrasted with the way of false (Pharisaic) discipleship with regard to almsgiving, praying, fasting, material possessions, and neighbors.

III. Conclusion

- 7.13–23: Jesus gives three warnings, which contrast the two ways of discipleship and indicate the seriousness of the demand of 5:20.
- 7:24–27: Matthew's final saying, which serves as a summary of his meaning, likens the doer to one who builds on rock and the nondoer to one who builds on sand. The meaning is clear: discipleship demands not just talking, but doing.

In this discourse, Matthew indicates his understanding of Christian discipleship, which he constantly illustrates throughout the rest of the Gospel. The true disciple, unlike the Pharisees, not only teaches the law but "does" the law. He not only does the law, but he does "all" of the law; that is, the true disciple governs his life by the radical kingdom will of God. The true disciple recognizes that the law of love is the principle of interpretation and discernment for all laws. Finally, the true disciple is one who lives through faith, a complete and wholehearted trust in God.

Jesus' wisdom teaching is illustrated in his many quotable sayings. In a culture that relied primarily on oral communication, important ideas had to be expressed in memorable formulas or they would be quickly forgotten. Once forgotten, they would be lost forever. The parables reveal that Jesus possessed a poetic sensitivity, and many of his stories demonstrate his clever wit.

The remembered sayings of Jesus could not remain free-floating in the Gospel narratives but occur in particular situations that offer clues about their interpretations. The Gospel writers shaped many of Jesus' sayings into "pronouncement stories." These are structured as brief incidents that climax when Jesus delivers a terse one-liner for which the opponent has no response. Many of these zingers are so familiar that even today many people can quote them ("Give to Caesar what is Caesar's, and to God what is God's" or "The poor you always have with you") even though they have no clue about the Gospel incidents from which they come. Mark 2:15–28 contains three stories that end with Jesus' pronouncements about dining with sinners, fasting, and Sabbath observance.

Besides these brief pronouncement stories, Jesus' wisdom is demonstrated in many controversy stories in which Jesus is challenged and argues with his opponents (see p. 161). These incidents are triggered by the behavior of Jesus and his

WHAT CAN YOU DO?

disciples, the cures and signs Jesus performs, or the questions that his opponents ask. Recall that in their culture, men constantly engaged in the public testing of one another to acquire honor at the expense of others. Every public question challenged the honor and reputation of the teacher. So Jesus' answers in these stories not only illustrated his clever mind at work but increased his status in the eyes of his audience.

JESUS IN CONTROVERSY WITH THE PHARISEES
(MATTHEW 22:15–22)

Then the Pharisees went and plotted to entrap him in what he said. So they sent their disciples to him, along with the Herodians, saying, "Teacher, we know that you are sincere, and teach the way of God in accordance with truth, and show deference to no one; for you do not regard people with partiality. Tell us, then, what you think. Is it lawful to pay taxes to the emperor, or not?" But Jesus, aware of their malice, said, "Why are you putting me to the test, you hypocrites? Show me the coin used for the tax." And they brought him a denarius. Then he said to them, "Whose head is this, and whose title?" They answered, "The emperor's." Then he said to them, "Give therefore to the emperor the things that are the emperor's, and to God the things that are God's." When they heard this, they were amazed; and they left him and went away.

The controversy stories also demonstrate that not all of Jesus' wisdom fit into the conventional molds. Through his

wisdom teaching and his miracles, Jesus offered a new awareness of the mysterious presence of the hidden God who is luring
us into a life-changing relationship. Jesus' wisdom offered his
followers a new worldview—a new vision of reality, new values
to order and guide their lives, and new behaviors that ought to
reorder their lives if they join his kingdom community.

The wise person knew the way the world worked and the
right way to live/walk with God. Israelite wisdom proposed a
worldview that included an intellectual organization of the
world (a way of seeing) and cues for deciding on the right values
and behaviors (a way of being). The memorable formulas of the
proverbs, for example, are not just convenient ways to store and
retrieve knowledge but shape a worldview by furnishing
categories, names, rules, roles, and the accumulated results of
hard-won experience that helped one master the complexities of
everyday life. Jesus' kingdom worldview and its lifestyle provide
the context in which the meaning of life in relation to God and
others can emerge. His way of seeing the world and of being and
acting in it suggest a new way of interpreting the events in our
lives. In sketching out Jesus' religious worldview (one that
includes God and God's activity as an essential part of reality),
there are certain basic questions to answer.

Who Is God?

Jesus identifies God as the king, the all-powerful yet benevolent ruler of the cosmos and of history. Jesus' theology does not emphasize the distant, transcendent mystery of God but rather the activity of God in our world searching for a relationship with humanity.

God is benevolent (Heavenly Patron-Father). God is not hostile but is a generous and favorably disposed patron who is characterized as always doing what is best for all creatures, giving what they need and arranging all things for their good. God is a bountiful gift giver, a benefactor who does not hoard resources or the necessities for living. God is concerned with saving his clients from difficult situations and mending any breakdowns in the relationship.

God is the ruler (Patron-King-Lord) over the cosmos and of history. God's wisdom and power establish the sacred order for all reality. Nothing happens without God's knowledge and consent. As creator, God fills the world with good things and makes all fruitful. As ruler, God orders creation and directs whatever happens among the nations. God the almighty maintains this divine order as judge of creation, designating the appropriate rewards or punishments for disorder.

What Is God Doing?

God's presence and activity are always for the sake of relationships. God's purpose and plan are revealed in the drama of God's entering into a covenant with humanity. Thus human history is, at its core, salvation history—the story of God in search of a people who will form the kind of community that God envisions.

God's plan illustrates how the divine power is used to realize the right kind of relationships. As the familiar salvation story unfolds, God's patronal roles as life giver (creator), rescuer (savior), covenant maker (master), lawgiver and judge (lord) are played out in relation to the communities chosen as God's covenant partners. God's presence to judge (demonstrating God's ethical seriousness) and to save (demonstrating God's gracious mercy) transforms all creation.

But Jesus' alternative worldview suggests that, despite all efforts to implement the holiness agenda, Israel had failed to fulfill God's dream. A new community must be formed. Jesus' kingdom is the fulfillment of God's search for a community in which dominion would be held by God alone and the people would live in right relationships based on justice, held together by love, and providing the fullness of life for all.

Who Are We in Relation to God?

Because God's power and action are directed toward establishing a new covenant relationship, the disciples of Jesus are the people who are called to be in a new relationship with God. They are the new Israel. To symbolize this connection with the twelve tribes that constituted the original Israel, Jesus chose twelve disciples as the foundation of his kingdom (Mt 10:1–16; Mk 3:13–19; Lk 6:12–16). The evangelists' confusion over their exact names indicates that their symbolic function as the Twelve is more important than their individual identity.

Where Are We in God's Plan?

Just as we can use maps to discover our location and calendars to place ourselves in time, so in a religious worldview we must know where we are in relation to God's map of the cosmos and timetable for history. Jesus proclaimed that he and his audience lived at the moment of the final transformation of all reality according to God's plan. Jesus imagines and describes this reordered world as the kingdom of God and invites us to cooperate with God in its realization. He described this as a new age (Mt 19:28, NAB) when the right order desired by God would be established.

What Is Wrong?

If you ask people what is wrong with our world, you get answers like the economy, or politics, or the breakdown of family values, or lax moral standards. If you asked Jesus, his answer was sin. Jesus reminded us that our world and our history are dominated by evil powers rather than by God, and hence right relationships are impaired.

Because God aims to establish the right kind of relationships, sin can be generically described as whatever breaks down relationships. Specific Hebrew words for sin describe particular ways to weaken and dissolve relationships—

rebellion, disobedience, deviation from the way, missing the mark, breaking the law. The disorder created by sin is characterized as evil, folly, alienation, and abomination.

Jesus proposes a worldview that affirms that our real enemies are the evil powers contesting against God for world dominance and demanding our loyalty. Consequently our world is a battleground of good and evil powers locked in a life-and-death struggle for mastery. Because human sinfulness constantly breaks down our relationships with God and one another, the history of our world has been the story of the gradual and insidious domination of evil instead of the triumph of the kingdom of God.

Evil has slowly but surely set up an alternative order to God's divine order and rule over the world. Human empires personify the disorder and domination of sin. Through human empires, evil has created an alternative order for our world that directly contradicts God's desire for the right kind of community. The signs of this sinful dominance are evident in the chaos plaguing our cosmos, our history, our communities, and ourselves.

What Is the Solution?

The solution for what is wrong must be directly related to the problem. The remedy for relationships broken by sin is restoration to harmony. The generic description of this harmony is salvation. The metaphor of health is the source of our term for salvation (Latin, *salus*, meaning "health"). Before *salvation* became a technical theological term, it meant to rescue someone from a difficult situation. So salvation comes when a rescuer (redeemer) or saver (savior) comes to help those in need.

The biblical concept of salvation describes God stepping in to remedy the breakdown of the relationship between God and humanity. Humans, who are subject to the seductive powers of evil, introduce disorder into God's creation through their sin. Their sin breaks down relationships. But because God originally invited and established the relationship, God must act to restore what has been broken down. Salvation history is the story of God's interventions not only to establish relationships but also to restore them when they inevitably break down because of human sin.

Jesus proclaimed that he and his message were the remedy for the disordered relationships that have plagued humanity since its beginning. As God's Messiah, Son, and end-times agent, Jesus inaugurates the kingdom of right relationships in which evil and its harmful effects (sickness, disease, suffering, and death) will dominate our lives no more. Because the coming of the kingdom will establish healthy relationships, its arrival can be symbolized by physical healing and be described as the forgiveness of sins, that is, eliminating whatever has broken down the relationship.

Jesus the Wonder Worker

Jesus' deeds of power are directly related to his kingdom worldview. They are the first signs that God is breaking the stranglehold of Satan on our world. Jesus shared Gods'

JESUS' SHORTEST SERMON (LUKE 4:15–24)

He began to teach in their synagogues and was praised by everyone.
When he came to Nazareth, where he had been brought up,
he went to the synagogue on the sabbath day, as was his custom.
He stood up to read, and the scroll of the prophet Isaiah was given
to him. He unrolled the scroll and found the place where it was
written:

> *"The Spirit of the Lord is upon me,*
> *because he has anointed me*
> *to bring good news to the poor.*
> *He has sent me to proclaim release to the captives*
> *and recovery of sight to the blind,*
> *to let the oppressed go free,*
> *to proclaim the year of the Lord's favor."*

And he rolled up the scroll, gave it back to the attendant, and sat down. The eyes of all in the synagogue were fixed on him. Then he began to say to them, "Today this scripture has been fulfilled in your hearing." All spoke well of him and were amazed at the gracious words that came from his mouth. They said, "Is not this Joseph's son?" He said to them, "Doubtless you will quote to me this proverb, 'Doctor, cure yourself!' And you will say, 'Do here also in your hometown the things that we have heard you did at Capernaum.'" And he said, "Truly I tell you, no prophet is accepted in the prophet's hometown."

WHAT CAN YOU DO?

power to do the work of God by feeding the hungry, healing the sick, and opening the kingdom community to everyone.

Although we use the word *miracles* to describe these events, the biblical writers used the terms *deeds of power* (Mt 7:22; 11:20–23; 13:54, 58; Mk 6:2, 5, 14; 9:39; Lk 10:13; 19:37), *signs* (Mt 24:24; Mk 13:22; Jn 2:11, 23; 20:30), and *wonders* (Jn 4:48). Their importance was not primarily in what happened but rather in their symbolic value. Like Jesus' parables and meals, Jesus' cures, exorcisms, resuscitations, and nature wonders are signs of God's presence breaking into our world to change it forever.

Signs and wonders were not absent from the Old Testament. However, they occurred primarily in three important periods when the crucial issue of God's power to save the people was put to the test:

- at the time of exodus from Egypt
- in the ninth century B.C., when the kingdom was confronted with a choice of worshiping the Jewish God Yahweh or the false gods of their neighbors
- during the Maccabean revolt against their Greek overlords (168–164 B.C.)

In each period, the people's desperate situation was answered by Yahweh's action through extraordinary events that were both acts and at the same time pointers to an even greater salvation to come.

JESUS' DEEDS OF POWER (MIRACLES)

Exorcisms	Mark	Matthew	Luke	John
the blind mute	___	12:22–23	11:14–15	___
the Gerasene demon	5:1–20	8:28–34	8:26–39	___
the Greek woman's daughter	7:24–30	15:21–28	___	___
the man with a mute demon	___	9:32–34	___	___
the boy with a mute demon	9:14–29	17:14–20	9:37–43	___
the unclean demon at Capernaum	1:23–28	___	4:33–37	___
Healings				
the afflicted woman	___	___	13:10–17	___
blind Bartimaeus	10:46–52	20:29–34	18:35–43	___
the blind man of Bethsaida	8:22–26	___	___	___
the centurion's slave/son	___	8:5–13	7:1–10	4:45–54
the crippled woman	___	___	13:11–13	___
the deaf-mute	7:31–37	___	___	___
the high priest's servant	___	___	22:50–51	___
a leper	1:40–45	8:1–4	5:12–16	___
the man with a withered hand	3:1–6	12:9–14	6:6–11	___
the man born blind	___	___	___	9:1–7
the man with dropsy	___	___	14:1–6	___
many at Peter's house	1:29–34	8:14–17	4:38–41	___

Jesus' Deeds of Power

From this Old Testament perspective, Jesus' signs and wonders suggested that his time was again a desperate situation when God would act. However, the astounding surprise that God would act definitively in and through Jesus would be understood only after his resurrection. In Jesus the final battle between God and Satan for domination of the world reached its resolution.

Healings	Mark	Matthew	Luke	John
a paralytic	2:1–12	9:1–8	5:17–26	
the paralytic by the pool				5:1–9
Peter's mother-in-law	1:29–31	8:14–15	4:38–39	
the ten lepers			17:11–19	
the two blind men		9:27–31		
the woman with a blood flow	5:24–34	9:20–22	8:42–48	

Resuscitations

	Mark	Matthew	Luke	John
Jairus's daughter	5:21–24, 35–43	9:18–19, 23–26	8:40–42, 49–55	
Lazarus				11:1–44
the widow's son at Nain			7:11–17	

Nature wonders

	Mark	Matthew	Luke	John
a fish with a coin		17:24–27		
five thousand sharing loaves and fish	6:35–44	14:15–21	9:12–17	6:1–15
four thousand sharing loaves and fish	8:1–10	15:32–39		
the stilling of a storm	4:35–41	8:23–27	8:22–25	21:1–11
an unusual catch of fish			5:1–11	
walking on water	6:47–52	14:24–33		6:16–21
water into wine				2:1–11
the withering fig tree	11:12–14, 20–25	21:18–22		

Like a deadly virus attacking God's creation, Satan's disordering power had affected the order of the natural world through the chaos of storms, famine, plagues, and other disasters. It affected the social order through the hatred that erupted in family feuds and national wars, rebellion against authority, and the breakdown of community relationships. It also affected the bodily order through sickness, disease, and finally, death.

Jesus' deeds of power signified that God was reordering each of these realms. Satan's domination of the world and the evil agenda of disorder could not match God's power and the divine agenda of right order (salvation, healing in all its dimensions). Jesus' various signs—exorcisms, cures, resuscitations, and nature miracles—demonstrated that Satan had lost control and God was now in control.

Jesus of Nazareth was the most scientific man that ever trod the globe. He plunged beneath the material surface of things, and found the spiritual cause.

—*MARY BAKER EDDY*
(1821–1910), founder of the Church of Christ Scientist

Jesus' exorcisms showed God's kingdom had come. The evil spirits that had taken possession of persons to instigate evil were driven out. Though some of Jesus' audience interpreted his exorcisms as the work of Satan, Jesus explained that this was absurd. Why would Satan drive out his helpers? No, the key was that a stronger power—God—was now at work and the weaker power of evil could not hold on to its hard-won spoils (Mt 12:29; Mk 3:27; Lk 10:18; 11:14–26).

Jesus' cures pointed to God's transforming power already at work in our degenerating and dying bodies. Jesus was a healer for all those in his audience who suffered the ravages of poor physical, mental, and spiritual health. Like a magnet, Jesus drew the poor, the outcasts, the sick, the lepers, the mute, the blind, and the lame to himself for healing and inclusion into his new community. The ambiguity of the Greek word for "save/heal" allowed Luke to emphasize that physical and spiritual health are interconnected. When Jesus tells those he cures, "Your faith has saved you," this could also mean "Your faith has healed you" (Lk 7:50; 8:48; 17:19; 18:42).

Jesus, on whom be peace, has said: "The world is a bridge: Pass over it, but do not build your dwelling there."

—Arabic inscription on a city gate in Fatepuhr-Sikri, India (1601)

Jesus' resuscitations of the dead indicated that God's power is always at work to give life. Death was the final triumph of evil. For the ancients, evil infiltrated bodies as sickness and progressed until the disorder got so great that a person died. By bringing the comatose daughter of Jairus back to life (Mt 9:18–26; Mk 5:21–43; Lk 8:40–56), restoring the only son to a widow at Nain (Lk 7:11–17), and inviting his beloved friend Lazarus to come out of the grave (Jn 11), Jesus confirmed that God's life-giving power had triumphed over the death-dealing power of evil.

Jesus' nature wonders demonstrate God's power over creation (the stilling of the storm, Mt 8:18, 23–37; Mk 4:35–41; Lk 8:22–25; the feeding of the five thousand, Mt 14:13–21; Mk 6:32–44; Lk 9:11–17; Jn 6:5–13; the feeding of the four thousand, Mt 15:32–39; Mk 8:1–10; the walking on

JESUS' WONDROUS DEEDS

Jesus' deeds of power, which we usually call miracles, are signs of God's power to reorder our world from the destructive effects of sin. Like the Israelite prophets before him, Jesus did not perform miracles for his own advantage or to prove anything. Rather, his miracles were ways in which he did the work of God—by healing the sick, he protected people from danger and threats to life; by feeding the hungry, he provided sustenance; by performing exorcisms and controlling nature, he ordered creation properly in relation to God. Of themselves, miracles are not proof of anything. But they are certainly wonderful signs for those who have "eyes to see."

Through a careful study of the miracle stories, scholars have recognized that many of them follow a basic pattern that goes something like this:

1. the seriousness of the situation is reported

2. the wonder-worker comes to the scene

3. the deed of power is performed

4. the audience who witnesses the event responds

This fourfold pattern is illustrated in the deeds of power related on pp. 175 and 177–178.

---

the water, Mt 14:22–33; Mk 6:45–52; Jn 6:16–21; the cursing of the fig tree, Mt 21:18–22; Mk 11:12–14; Lk 13:6–9; the catch of fish, Lk 5:1–11; Jn 21:1–14; and the change of water into wine, Jn 2:1–12).

Jesus Restores a Widow's Only Son to Life (Luke 7:11–16)

Soon afterwards he went to a town called Nain, and his disciples
and a large crowd went with him. As he approached the gate of
the town, a man who had died was being carried out. He was his
mother's only son, and she was a widow; and with her was a large
crowd from the town. When the Lord saw her, he had compassion
for her and said to her, "Do not weep." Then he came forward
and touched the bier, and the bearers stood still. And he said,
"Young man, I say to you, rise!" The dead man sat up and began
to speak, and Jesus gave him to his mother. Fear seized all of
them; and they glorified God, saying, "A great prophet has risen
among us!" and "God has looked favorably on his people!"

Deciphering a Miracle

The word *miracle* refers to that which causes wonder. The
extraordinary is one essential element in a miracle, as the
observers of Jesus' wonders so often illustrate through their
awe and astonishment. The other is that the extraordinary
event cannot be explained in terms of familiar, everyday
causation and so is attributed to a superhuman force. Everyone would readily conclude that a more-than-human power
would be necessary for a human to perform the miracle.

In reading the miracle stories, we notice that the usual
concern of Jesus' audience focused on the source of such
awesome power. They saw the event; they experienced the

wonder. The deed of power was not something beyond the natural world, but it opened the natural world beyond its ordinary workings. (For instance, Jesus did not pull bread out of thin air but took a few loaves and turned them into many.) They recognized that only through the influence of a supernatural power could the natural world be reordered. The question was whether this more-than-human agent was good (God) or evil (Satan), a benefactor or a tyrant.

Even for believers, miracles did not create faith but presupposed it. Miracles were not proofs but wonderful signs for those who had "eyes to see." Those who could not accept the miracles remained simply "astonished."

Miracles, like everything else we experience, are open to various interpretations and in fact always require them. The meaning of miracles is variable and always depends on the context in which one chooses to interpret them.

Thus, disputes about miracle claims were common in the Greco-Roman world, especially between competing social and religious groups. In a given situation, people had to decide whether or not an occurrence was a miracle. Was it an extraordinary happening that couldn't be explained in terms of familiar causes? Should it be attributed to divine power?

When his opponents accused him of being in league with Satan, Jesus asserted that because he did his wondrous deeds through God's power, they were signs pointing to the coming of the kingdom (Mt 12:22–30; Mk 3:22–27; Lk

11:14–23). They showed that God was rescuing the world and its inhabitants from the domination of Satan. The first skirmishes in the battle for the world had begun through Jesus' wondrous deeds, and God, the stronger one, would inevitably triumph.

JESUS EXORCISES A GERASENE MAN'S DEMON (MARK 5:1–20)

They came to the other side of the sea, to the country of the Gerasenes. And when he had stepped out of the boat, immediately a man out of the tombs with an unclean spirit met him. He lived among the tombs; and no one could restrain him any more, even with a chain; for he had often been restrained with shackles and chains, but the chains he wrenched apart, and the shackles he broke in pieces; and no one had the strength to subdue him. Night and day among the tombs and on the mountains he was always howling and bruising himself with stones. When he saw Jesus from a distance, he ran and bowed down before him; and he shouted at the top of his voice, "What have you to do with me, Jesus, Son of the Most High God? I adjure you by God, do not torment me." For he had said to him, "Come out of the man, you unclean spirit!" Then Jesus asked him, "What is your name?" He replied, "My name is Legion; for we are many." He begged him earnestly not to send them out of the country. Now there on the hillside a great herd of swine was feeding; and the unclean spirits begged him, "Send us into the swine; let us enter them." So he gave them permission. And the unclean spirits came out and entered

the swine; and the herd, numbering about two thousand, rushed
down the steep bank into the sea, and were drowned in the sea.

The swineherds ran off and told it in the city and in the
country. Then people came to see what it was that had happened.
They came to Jesus and saw the demoniac sitting there, clothed
and in his right mind, the very man who had had the legion; and
they were afraid. Those who had seen what had happened to the
demoniac and to the swine reported it. Then they began to beg
Jesus to leave their neighborhood. As he was getting into the boat,
the man who had been possessed by demons begged him that he
might be with him. But Jesus refused, and said to him, "Go home
to your friends, and tell them how much the Lord has done for
you, and what mercy he has shown you." And he went away and
began to proclaim in the Decapolis how much Jesus had done for
him; and everyone was amazed.

Miracles: Then and Now

The ancient interpretation of Jesus' signs and wonders con-
trasts starkly with the way we have been taught to approach
miracles through modern science. Our struggle with miracles
stems primarily from the limitations of our self-imposed
scientific worldview. When science determines what can be
extraordinary and, hence, miraculous, the religious meaning
of miracles is diluted.

For the last three centuries, as science became synonymous with what can be known, and the scientific method

of thinking with human reason, scientists separated reality into the natural order (the material, observable, measurable reality known by scientific methods) and the supernatural order (the immaterial, unobservable, unmeasurable reality known by an irrational leap of faith). Because miracles belonged to the supernatural order, they were described as scientific anomalies that were contrary to the verifiable laws of nature (at least as scientists had determined nature must act).

[Jesus was a person] whose rage of compassion was founded on a very accurate social analysis, and issued not only in an outpouring of immediate healing and personal liberation, but in the creation of an alternative model of relationship between believers and between God and humankind.

—*ROSEMARY HOUGHTON,*
theologian, "Godly Anger and Beyond," in *The Way* (April 1990)

These scientists presupposed that the world was a closed system in which only the "material" and scientifically verifiable were natural. The laws of nature were always consistent and constant; thus natural causes had to account for everything that occurred. While this approach was more true for eighteenth- and nineteenth-century science, twentieth-century scientists were much more hesitant to assume the constancy of natural laws, especially after the surprising discovery of subatomic particles that acted in ways far different from what scientists predicted based on their previous knowledge.

But it is impossible to understand the religious significance of Jesus' miracles by viewing them through the lens of science and identifying them as violations of the rules of natural order. This concept of nature and natural laws is foreign to the religious worldview of the Bible. In that time and culture, people understood the world to be open to influences from beings of a higher order.

JESUS EXORCISES A GREEK WOMAN'S DAUGHTER (MARK 7:24–30)

From there he set out and went away to the region of Tyre. He entered a house and did not want anyone to know he was there. Yet he could not escape notice, but a woman whose little daughter had an unclean spirit immediately heard about him, and she came and bowed down at his feet.

Now the woman was a Gentile, of Syrophoenician origin. She begged him to cast the demon out of her daughter.

He said to her, "Let the children be fed first, for it is not fair to take the children's food and throw it to the dogs."

But she answered him, "Sir, even the dogs under the table eat the children's crumbs."

Then he said to her, "For saying that, you may go—the demon has left your daughter."

So she went home, found the child lying on the bed, and the demon gone.

WHAT CAN YOU DO?

We don't need to be limited by the scientific worldview. We don't have to identify reason with scientific reason or reality with only the material world. When we allow that there is a world beyond what can be scientifically perceived and explained, we are in a position to look more deeply into Jesus' miracles. In this way, the believer's world is much more mysterious than the world as it has thus far been defined by science.

Like Jesus and the people of his time, believers recognize that reality is much more open to influences of powers greater than themselves. If this is the course we choose, then Jesus' deeds of power challenge us to answer the question that his contemporaries asked: From what source does a human person acquire the power to do such extraordinary things? What, indeed, do such extraordinary deeds *mean*?

Learning from Jesus: Lifelong Conversion

Jesus not only proclaimed that God was the ruler of our world, but he demonstrated by his signs and wonders how God's rule would reorder everything that was now broken and disordered through sin. Jesus' signs and wonders showed that God's salvation was available for all. His worldview invited people to see their ordinary world in a new way and to live accordingly.

Embracing Jesus' worldview has several consequences. Because one's worldview influences values, which in turn impact behavior, adopting Jesus' worldview and living it require the change of heart and mind that Jesus called repentance, or conversion (Mt 4:17; Mk 1:15; Lk 5:32). Hearing and heeding Jesus' kingdom message will challenge every dimension of our relationships with God and others.

Jesus' kingdom invitation challenges us to notice God in our midst and make a commitment to relate to God. It challenges us to see the world as God does, evaluate it as God does, and act in it as God does. It challenges us to link our hope for a new order with God's dream for the right kind of community. Finally, it challenges us to engage in the real power struggle between God and Satan, good and evil.

Because worldviews tend to be exclusive, adopting Jesus' kingdom worldview demands a rejection of all other worldviews. To affirm its truth makes other worldviews either untrue or irrelevant. As an alternative worldview, the kingdom worldview affirms that, through Jesus the Christ, God has initiated the final transformation of our sinfully disordered world into God's reordered world.

If we choose to follow Jesus, all of our power and effort must be directed to realizing this new kingdom community. This new creation will be characterized by justice (God enters to secure right relations), love (God bonds us in solidarity and covenant friendship), the absence of evil (God triumphs over evil), and the absence of the sting of death (God offers new life where there is no hope of life). This new world order will bring about universal peace.

JESUS HEALS A CRIPPLED WOMAN
(LUKE 13:10–17)

Now he was teaching in one of the synagogues on the sabbath. And just then there appeared a woman with a spirit that had crippled her for eighteen years. She was bent over and was quite unable to stand up straight. When Jesus saw her, he called her over and said, "Woman, you are set free from your ailment." When he laid his hands on her, immediately she stood up straight and began praising God. But the leader of the synagogue, indignant because Jesus had cured on the sabbath, kept saying to the crowd, "There are six days on which work ought to be done; come on those days and be cured, and not on the sabbath day." But the Lord answered him and said, "You hypocrites! Does not each of you on the sabbath untie his ox or his donkey from the manger, and lead it away to give it water? And ought not this woman, a daughter of Abraham whom Satan bound for eighteen long years, be set free from this bondage on the sabbath day?" When he said this, all his opponents were put to shame; and the entire crowd was rejoicing at all the wonderful things that he was doing.

But this new order will be impossible unless we learn from the wisdom of Jesus. Vatican Council II (1962–1965) reminded us that "wisdom gently attracts the human mind to a quest and a love for what is true and good. Steeped in wisdom, persons pass through visible realities to those which are unseen. Our era needs such wisdom more than bygone ages if human discoveries are to be further humanized. For the future of the world stands in peril unless wiser persons are forthcoming" (*The Church in the Modern World*, #15, modified Abbot translation).

In acting out his royal role, Jesus' strategy of wise words and deeds of power continue to draw our attention to God's powerful reordering of everyday life. They refuse to let us separate God from anywhere, from anyone, from anything that is happening to us. They invite us to wonder, to seek and discover the presence of the God who created us, sustains us, searches us out, and finds us to call us into a relationship that will never end.

JESUS TRANSFORMS WATER INTO WINE (JOHN 2:1–11)

On the third day there was a wedding in Cana of Galilee, and the mother of Jesus was there. Jesus and his disciples had also been invited to the wedding. When the wine gave out, the mother of Jesus said to him, "They have no wine." And Jesus said to her, "Woman, what concern is that to you and to me? My hour has not yet come." His mother said to the servants, "Do whatever he tells you." Now standing there were six stone water jars for the Jewish rites of purification, each holding twenty or thirty gallons. Jesus

WHAT CAN YOU DO?

said to them, "Fill the jars with water." And they filled them up
to the brim. He said to them, "Now draw some out, and take it to
the chief steward." So they took it. When the steward tasted the
water that had become wine, and did not know where it came
from (though the servants who had drawn the water knew), the
steward called the bridegroom and said to him, "Everyone serves
the good wine first, and then the inferior wine after the guests
have become drunk. But you have kept the good wine until now."

THE WONDROUS SHARING OF A YOUNG BOY'S LUNCH (JOHN 6:1–14)

After this Jesus went to the other side of the Sea of Galilee, also
called the Sea of Tiberias. A large crowd kept following him,
because they saw the signs that he was doing for the sick. Jesus
went up the mountain and sat down there with his disciples.
Now the Passover, the festival of the Jews, was near. When he
looked up and saw a large crowd coming toward him, Jesus said
to Philip, "Where are we to buy bread for these people to eat?"
He said this to test him, for he himself knew what he was going to
do. Philip answered him, "Six months' wages would not buy
enough bread for each of them to get a little." One of his disciples,
Andrew, Simon Peter's brother, said to him, "There is a boy here
who has five barley loaves and two fish. But what are they among
so many people?" Jesus said, "Make the people sit down." Now
there was a great deal of grass in the place; so they sat down,
about five thousand in all. Then Jesus took the loaves, and when
he had given thanks, he distributed them to those who were
seated; so also the fish, as much as they wanted. When they were

JESUS THE KING: REORDERING LIFE IN GOD'S PRESENCE

satisfied, he told his disciples, "Gather up the fragments left over, so that nothing may be lost." So they gathered them up, and from the fragments of the five barley loaves, left by those who had eaten, they filled twelve baskets. When the people saw the sign that he had done, they began to say, "This is indeed the prophet who is to come into the world."

WHAT CAN YOU DO?

Are you the only visitor to Jerusalem
who does not know of the things that
have taken place there in these days?

—LUKE 24:18

CHAPTER ELEVEN

Jesus Who Suffered and Died

The explanations we've sketched out so far of who Jesus was and what he was doing reflect the Christian interpretation. There were other interpretations about these crucial issues, and these differences ultimately led to the death of Jesus.

As with so much else about Jesus, the fact of his death pales in relation to what it meant. His death was not something tacked onto his life and ministry. Rather, it was the direct consequence of his claims; his aims; his roles as prophet, priest, and king; and his strategies of parables, meal sharing, and miracles.

Until a person dies, the meaning of his or her life remains open and changeable. But death brings a closure, and only then can the significance of a whole life be understood. In Jesus' case, his death was a direct result of how he lived and what he taught. So his death became the culminating point to which his whole life was directed. Only by examining his death and the circumstances surrounding it can we discover the richer meaning of his life and ministry. The account of these circumstances, the suffering, trials, and crucifixion of Jesus, are narrated by the Gospel writers in the sections of their Gospels that Scripture scholars call the Passion narratives.

Good Son or Rebel Son?

The conflicting interpretations about Jesus centered on his identity. Earlier we outlined the various relationships that provided the complex makeup of his identity as a human being, as the Jewish Messiah, as God's end-times agent, and finally as God's unique Son.

His opponents, however, offered alternative interpretations of these affiliations and the claims that accompanied them. True, Jesus was a human being, but he had no authority to assume the mantle of David and claim to be Messiah. Nor was there any evidence to suggest that this obscure carpenter was God's divine agent ushering in the final transformation as the Son of man. And most shameful of all was his claim to be God's Son. Grasping at this honor demonstrated how deluded Jesus was and how misguided his claims were.

It was impossible to resolve the conflict of interpretations over whether Jesus was a good and honorable son or a bad and rebellious one. Both groups, Jesus' disciples and his opponents, were certain that their view was right. Both also knew how they ought to act in light of their conclusions.

Jesus' disciples emulated him and were willing to follow him anywhere, even to death itself. Of course, they also hoped for the rewards of being in his retinue when God bestowed the expected favors on Jesus for his service to the kingdom.

His opponents, on the other hand, surely considered his reach for these honors to be dishonorable. It was one thing to struggle for honor against others in the rough-and-tumble competition of the marketplace. But it was another to assume for oneself honors that could only be bestowed by another, in this case God. Such disgraceful behavior demanded punishment.

The passion story becomes a parable of the community's own struggle in history. Jesus' sufferings are sober testimony to the cost of preaching the Gospel with integrity. His triumph over death is a guarantee that human suffering can be the birth pangs of a new creation.

—DONALD SENIOR, C.P.
Scripture scholar, *The Passion of Jesus in the Gospel of Mark*

Jewish law was clear about the punishment that ought to be handed out to a rebellious son. The same passage that first notes the rights and honors of the firstborn son then tells how to handle an incorrigible son.

JESUS WHO SUFFERED AND DIED

Instead of receiving honors, a rebellious son must be ostracized and killed. According to the Mosaic law in Deuteronomy, "If a man has a stubborn and unruly son who will not listen to his father or mother, and will not obey them even though they chastise him, his father and mother shall have him apprehended and brought out to the elders at the gate of his home city, where they shall say to those city elders, 'This son of ours is a stubborn and unruly fellow who will not listen to us; he is a glutton and a drunkard.' Then all his fellow citizens shall stone him to death. Thus shall you purge the evil from your midst, and all Israel, on hearing of it, shall fear" (Dt 21:18–21, NAB).

This citation indicates that an unruly son was an evil in the midst of the people and must be eradicated even if it means executing him as a lesson to others. Interestingly enough, Jesus was also accused of being a "glutton and a drunkard" (Mt 11:19; Lk 7:34). The Jewish high priest Caiaphas also calculated the benefit of Jesus' death for the people by counseling the Sanhedrin (the seventy-two-member council of elders) "that it is better for you to have one man die for the people than to have the whole nation destroyed" (Jn 11:50).

The conflict of interpretations was not limited to Jesus' identity as a good or rebellious son. It also extended to his behavior. Each of his roles was challenged by his Jewish opponents.

WHAT CAN YOU DO?

True or False Prophet?

From the Jewish perspective, Jesus' teaching led the people astray and created conflicting loyalties. Those who taught with authority, especially when they claimed to be prophets who spoke for God, were always being scrutinized. And just as an incorrigible son was to be killed as an example to purge evil from the community, so the same penalties held for false prophets.

The Jewish law was very clear that "if there arises among you a prophet or a dreamer who promises you a sign or wonder, urging you to follow other gods . . . pay no attention to the words of that prophet or that dreamer; for the Lord, your God, is testing you to learn whether you really love him with all your heart and with all your soul. . . . But that prophet or that dreamer shall be put to death, because . . . he has preached apostasy from the Lord. . . . Thus shall you purge the evil from your midst" (Dt 13:2–6, NAB).

The false prophet errs even more by assuming for himself a mission from God. Speaking through the prophet Jeremiah, God declared, "I am against those who prophesy lying dreams, says the Lord, and who tell them, and who lead my people astray by their lies and their recklessness, when I did not send them or appoint them; so they do not profit this people at all, says the Lord" (Jer 23:32).

Jesus' prophetic work, however, followed the ancient prophetic tradition. As one who was outside the official channels of power, Jesus proclaimed a message of God's presence in ordinary life and not just in the temple. God's presence demanded a rejection of sin and conversion of heart. Jesus' kingdom message, far from leading the people astray, was meant to call them back to the deepest covenant loyalty that was being forsaken through their sinful behavior.

True or False Priest?

Jesus' Jewish opponents also had a different interpretation about the meaning of his priestly task of gathering the kingdom community by sharing a common meal. They concluded that eating with sinners and others who were unclean defiled Jesus and created an unholy communion through the shared meal.

Like Buddha under the Bo tree, Jesus on his tree, has his eyes closed too. The difference is this. The pain and sadness of the world that Buddha's eyes close out is the pain and sadness of the world that the eyes of Jesus close in.

—*FREDERICK BUECHNER*
spiritual writer

Jesus, however, saw this communion with sinners as essential to his role as healer and to his eradication of the sin that broke down their relation to God and the community (Mt 9:12; Mk 2:17; Lk 5:31; 15:1–7). More than anything else, this mealtime communion demonstrated Jesus' break from the attitude of exclusion that stressed the holiness of God's chosen people. Jesus' meal sharing illustrated that God extended compassion and mercy to all people.

True or False King?

The king who claimed wisdom and used power for ruling over others could also turn into a tyrant whose wisdom became treacherous and his power volatile and dangerous. The conflict between Jesus (who appeared wise and just) and those who hated him had been previewed a hundred years earlier in the book of Wisdom (1:16–2:24).

In this startling passage, the rich and powerful flaunt their arrogant power by exploiting the just person. One of the main reasons for their hatred was that "he professes to have knowledge of God/and styles himself a child of the LORD" (Wis 2:13, NAB) and "boasts that God is his Father" (Wis 2:16, NAB). Their decision to kill the just one became an invitation for God to act, "for if the just one be the son of God, he will defend him/and deliver him from the hand of his foes" (Wis 2:18, NAB).

Jesus was recognized by his disciples as the messiah (Mt 16:21; Mk 8:29; Lk 9:20; Jn 6:69). But Jesus never seemed to accept their identification without some disclaimer that he would not be the political leader that they perhaps hoped for.

The claim of messianic kingship, as we will soon see, was also a particularly volatile claim in the Roman-occupied territory of Palestine.

In that world, the distinction between church and state, religion and politics was not sharply drawn. So every public religious claim could also have political ramifications. Although Jesus was not overtly aspiring to political power, any claim even remotely perceived by the Romans as a threat to their domination was swiftly and ruthlessly dealt with. For the Romans well knew that rebellion always smoldered in the hearts and minds of the people long before it ignited into open revolt.

Jesus' Passion: The Death of God's Honorable Son

The nagging conflict between Jesus and his Jewish opponents over his identity, mission, and ministry came to a head in the volatile events during the Passover in Jerusalem about the year A.D. 30 (or perhaps 33). The events of this week provide the framework for the story of Jesus' passion, that is, his suffering and death as narrated in the Gospels.

But we must note that these Gospel reports were written down about forty years or so after the events. And we must stress that they are reports, not eyewitness accounts. The reports agree in general but often differ in their arrangement of events and in many specific details. What is most clear about the various Passion accounts is that each one is tailored to the Gospel in which it appears and reinforces that particular Gospel writer's emphases about Jesus' identity and mission.

Mark was the first Gospel writer to gather the disparate elements in the Passion accounts and shape them into a coherent written narrative. Thus we could say that Mark "invented" the Passion story.

The term *invention* for the ancient writer like Mark and his audience did not mean that he just made it up out of his imagination. Rather, as every speaker and writer was taught, *invention* was a technical rhetorical term describing the skill of finding arguments that would persuade the audience. So we discover as we read Mark's Passion that it has been skillfully "invented" (in the rhetorical sense) to persuade his audience that Jesus was God's honorable Son. The other evangelists in turn follow Mark's insights. They tweak his arguments and highlight aspects of Jesus' identity that are important for their audiences. (Throughout the rest of the chapter, as Jesus' suffering and death are described, Scripture references are included from each Gospel, in case the reader wishes to follow the parallel stories.)

Before tracing the events of the Passion, we must recall that in their first-century culture the proper behavior for sons followed the expectations of clients to their patrons. Thus an honorable son would be characterized above all by his obedience, submission, unquestioning loyalty to his father and to the family, and scrupulous concern for the family honor. Any wavering of loyalty, defiance of the father's will, or rebellion against the father's plans would be regarded as openly shameful behavior that dishonored the son, the father, and the whole family.

The Triumphal Entry

Jesus' final week began with a great public demonstration of acclaim for him. In a gesture that could be seen as a prophetic sign of protest about the military role of the messiah, Jesus rode into Jerusalem on a donkey while people strewed palm fronds on his path (Mt 21:1–9; Mk 11:1–10; Lk 19:28–40).

He taught in the temple, reaching out one final time to his opponents and extending an invitation to conversion. He also performed another prophetic sign by disrupting the business going on in the temple (Mt 21:12–13; Mk 11:15–17; Lk 19:45–46). This sign was hardly a cleansing of the temple but instead a forewarning of God's judgment upon it and its consequent destruction when the end times came (Mt 24:1–36; Mk 13:1–37; Lk 21:5–36).

Jesus' Parable of the Dishonorable Tenants

During his final week of teaching in the temple area, Jesus told a parable that the Jewish chief priests, scribes, and elders clearly recognized was directed at them (Mk 12:1–12). The

WHAT CAN YOU DO?

placement of this parable is a clue to the meaning that Mark was trying to highlight about Jesus as God's honorable Son.

Jesus related how a man planted a vineyard (a common image for God's covenant people in the Old Testament) and leased it out to clients and went abroad. When their payment was due, the owner sent a servant to collect, but he was beaten. So the owner sent another and another, but the dishonorable clients beat, and even killed, some of the messengers.

Finally the exasperated owner decided that he would send his "beloved son" because certainly the clients would show him the proper honor and respect. But the clients decide to kill the son and heir so that the vineyard would be all theirs.

Then Jesus asked the audience what an honorable owner would do in response to such unbelievably shameful behavior by the clients. The immediate answer, of course, was that he would not tolerate such abuse of his honor. He would certainly come to destroy these wicked clients and give the vineyard to others. The Jewish leaders recognized that Jesus was telling this parable against them, and they wanted him killed. Later Christian readers of the Gospel would use this parable to interpret the death of Jesus as the initiation of a new covenant and the Christian community as the new people of God who would tend the vineyard in the proper way.

The Final Supper

Jesus' final supper is portrayed by Mark, Matthew, and Luke as the celebration of the Jewish Passover meal (Mt 26:1–35; Mk 14:1–31; Lk 22:1–38). John follows a slightly different calendar that puts the Passover one day later (Jn 13:1–38). The significance of the meal is highlighted either way. Passover was the great event of the Jewish people's deliverance. As Jesus celebrated with his followers, he had a premonition that this might be his last meal with them.

Jesus shifted the meaning of the meal into something no one expected. He told the disciples that he would be with them again whenever they celebrated this meal in his memory. But his presence would not merely be in memory but rather in the tangible elements of food and drink. The bread and wine would be his body and blood. And just as the wheat and grape die to become food and drink for sustaining earthly life, so Jesus dies to become food for eternal life.

During the meal, Jesus gave another sign that demonstrated how offering oneself for others must take place. Although he was their master and lord, like a slave or servant Jesus washed the feet of the disciples as a lesson for them to imitate. They would no longer be servants but "friends" (Jn 15:15).

But the meal was also clouded by the intimation that one of his own disciples, Judas, would betray him and that another, Peter, would deny him three times before sunup.

This betrayal and denial—the most shameful behaviors of a friend—stand in glaring contrast to the loyal behavior of Jesus the honorable Son.

Gethsemane

Jesus and the disciples left the supper and walked through the moonlit night to the Mount of Olives. In an olive grove known as Gethsemane, Jesus moved apart to pray. The content of his prayer as reported by Mark was similar to that expressed in the Lord's Prayer found in Matthew and Luke.

In the swirling events of the week, Jesus must have known that the hostility of his opponents had driven them to find a way to kill him (Mt 26:1–5; Mk 3:6; 11:18–19; Lk 19:47–48; Jn 11:47–53). But the real challenge was within his own heart. Was his death the price he must pay for the coming of God's kingdom? Could he remain obedient and loyal to his Father and the kingdom despite this demand?

Three times Jesus prayed that the suffering be removed but realized that this was not possible. So three times he repeated the prayer of a good Son who promised obedience to his Father's will despite the suffering it would bring (Mt 26:36–46; Mk 14:32–42; Lk 22:39–46; Jn 18:1).

Jesus' Betrayal and Arrest

When Jesus' prayer was finished, Judas came with an armed guard to arrest Jesus (Mt 26:47–56; Mk 14:43–52;

Lk 22:47–53; Jn 18:2–12). The predicted betrayal now became a reality. The betrayer's disloyalty was even more shameful because the sign marking Jesus for death was a kiss of friendship. In loyalty to his Father's plan, Jesus prohibited any use of violence to escape. In loyalty to his disciples, he bargained for their freedom.

Jesus' "Trial"

After his arrest, Jesus was taken to the Jewish leaders for a hearing (Mt 26:57–68; Mk 14:53–65; Lk 22:54–71; Jn 18:13–24). Although this is often called a trial, the ancients had far less sophisticated trial procedures regarding introducing evidence and the testimony and cross-examination of witnesses than we are used to today. Moreover, the evangelists reported what happened in a nontechnical way, as people might do if called upon to summarize what was going on in a celebrated trial today.

But again we must note that Mark arranged the incidents both in a logical way—arrest, hearing, verdict—and in a rhetorical way to advance his argument. Jesus' declaration to the high priest that he is God's Son is immediately followed by Peter's three denials that he even knows Jesus. The predicted denial now becomes a reality. Jesus' loyalty to his Father, his honorable silence, and truthful response to questions is starkly contrasted with Peter's disloyalty, cowardice, and lying.

Accusations by the Jewish Leaders

The interests of the Jewish leaders were both religious and political. Their zealous monotheism and refusal to tolerate other gods had more than once brought them into conflict with their Roman overlords. Loyalties to God and Caesar did not coexist very well. Jesus was taken before the Jewish leaders, and witnesses were brought forward. They accused him of terrorist activity: "We heard him say, 'I will destroy this temple that is made with hands, and in three days I will build another, not made with hands'" (Mk 14:58; Mt 26:61). Jesus the honorable Son was silent and made no response to these false accusations.

It is no accident that the charges of the Jewish leaders focused on the issue of the temple. Through his prophetic, priestly, and kingly service to God's presence in the ordinary realities of everyday life, Jesus stressed that God's presence was not confined to, or even primarily located, in the temple. Consequently, access to God through miracle and meal was not restricted to this building, its priesthood, and its ceremonies. The threat that Jesus' teachings posed to the temple-centered religion created much of the hostility that led to Jesus' death.

When the testimony of the witnesses did not agree and the charges were evaporating, the high priest formulated the issue as a direct question about Jesus' identity as the Christ, the Son of God. Jesus affirmed these two claims and added

JESUS WHO SUFFERED AND DIED

the missing component. He was also the Son of man, whose work for God to usher in the final kingdom would soon be rewarded with heavenly exaltation (Mt 26:63–64; Mk 14:61–62; Lk 22:67–70). Here at the crucial moment of his life, when the life-and-death issue was his identity, Jesus affirmed the three most important sonships that defined who he was.

The Jews were shocked and considered this claim blasphemy, which was punishable by death. But because they did not have the power to execute Jesus (Jn 18:31), they had to take their case to the Roman governor, Pontius Pilate (Lk 3:1), who was in residence in Jerusalem during the Passover festival. Pilate's presence at that time was a precaution because he knew well that when large numbers of Jews congregated, their religious zeal could trigger political rebellion.

Accusations by the Roman Governor

The key claim about Jesus that would catch Pilate's attention was certainly that of messiah, interpreted in a political way as king. Any claim to kingship was a direct challenge to the rule of Caesar. So when the Jewish leaders dragged Jesus to Pilate, they quickly focused their accusation on Jesus' "perverting our nation, forbidding us to pay taxes to the emperor, and saying that he himself is the Messiah, a king" (Lk 23:2).

Jesus, the noble son, would not respond to their slanderous accusations, but truthfully responded to Pilate's direct

WHAT CAN YOU DO?

question about his identity as "King of the Jews" (Mt 27:11–14; Mk 15:2–5; Lk 23:2–5). Pilate found no crime in this. Luke reports that the Jews then charged that he "stirs up the people by teaching throughout all Judea, from Galilee where he began even to this place" (Lk 23:5).

The Crucified becomes one with the unrecognized and misused and cruelly treated in every age. The nail-pierced Figure on Calvary haunts our race as a symbol of what is forever taking place generation after generation, and of what each of us has his part in.

—*HENRY SLOANE COFFIN*
theologian and pastor, *The Meaning of the Cross*

When Pilate realized that Jesus was a Galilean and that the situation was getting more volatile, he sent Jesus to Herod (Antipas), the son of Herod the Great, who was the Roman-appointed king for Galilee. This was the Herod who had beheaded John the Baptist (Mt 14:3–12; Mk 6:17–29; Lk 3:19–20) and had once wanted to kill Jesus (Lk 13:31–33). When sent to Herod, who was eager to meet Jesus and perhaps even see him do some sign or wonder, Jesus kept a noble silence. Because silence is always ambiguous and in need of interpretation, Herod concluded that Jesus was a fool, found nothing to condemn, and sent him back to Pilate (Lk 23:6–12).

In John's Gospel, the dialogue with Pilate reveals how all the participants were forced to choose their loyalties. After Jesus assured Pilate that his kingdom was not a worldly one,

Pilate declared him innocent but, with inscrutable Roman logic, then had him beaten. Then the religious establishment's real charge against Jesus surfaced. The Jews cry out, "We have a law, and according to that law he ought to die, because he made himself the Son of God" (Jn 19:7, NAB).

Full of fear at this revelation, Pilate questioned Jesus about his origins. Jesus then remained silent. When Pilate threatened him by claiming power over him, Jesus showed his loyalty and trust of his heavenly Father by reminding Pilate that his power was only from those above him. Pilate wanted to release Jesus, but Jesus' enemies played their trump card.

In the Roman social situation, loyalty to one's patron was the highest honor that a client could offer. Clients prided themselves on their relationship to powerful patrons and styled themselves "friends" even though there remained great inequality in their relationship. To deny one's loyalty reduced the supposed friend to a conniving traitor. Pilate, who owed his governorship to his relationship with his "friend" the emperor, was now put in a dilemma.

Pilate's various attempts to release Jesus were completely stymied when the people cried out, "If you release this man, you are no friend of the emperor. Everyone who claims to be a king sets himself against the emperor" (Jn 19:12). Now the test of loyalty confronted Pilate, who chose loyalty to the emperor over justice and truth. Wanting to be rid of the whole affair, Pilate handed Jesus over to the crowd for crucifixion.

But Jewish loyalty was also tested. When Pilate asked the Jewish leaders, "'Shall I crucify your King?' The chief priests answered, 'We have no king but the emperor'" (Jn 19:15). This reply is laced with woeful irony because throughout their history the Jewish people had consistently recognized God alone as their King (Pss 47:1–9; 74:12; 145:1; Jer 10:10; Ez 20:33) and lived with the tension of a human king who infringed on God's kingship (Jgs 8:23; 1 Sm 8:7; 12:12). By rejecting Jesus and pledging their loyalty to the Roman emperor, the Gospel writers suggest, the Jews rejected God as their king and cut themselves off from the kingdom God was inaugurating through him.

Jesus or Barabbas?

In an effort to have Jesus released, Pilate appealed to a custom of freeing a prisoner at festival time. So he put to the crowd the choice of Jesus, the so-called King of the Jews, or Barabbas, a notorious rebel whose terrorist activities included robbery and murder. Some manuscripts indicate that his name was Jesus Barabbas. In any case, the crowd called for Barabbas's release and Jesus' crucifixion (Mt 27:15–23; Mk 15:6–14; Lk 23:17–23; Jn 18:39–40).

This choice was also highly symbolic. The name *Barabbas* means "son of the father" (Aramaic, *Abba*). In his prayer of submission in Gethsemane, Jesus had used this term to address God as his Father (Mk 14:36). Although in the past this term has commonly been explained as the familiar address of a little child to "daddy," scholars now suggest that it means simply "father," as the evangelists always translate in their Greek. Although it seems more formal to us, nevertheless it carried all the emotional overtones of the father/son relationship.

John summarizes the meaning of the Passion from the viewpoint of the crowd. They were faced with the choice of Jesus, whose words and works demonstrate that he was the genuine "Son of the Father," or Barabbas, whose name claimed the association but whose violent deeds served only to break down and fragment God's community. Their loyalty led them to the false Barabbas.

Mockery

The mockery directed at Jesus was intended to humiliate and shame him for his claims of being a Jewish prophet and messiah-king. The Jewish leaders mocked him for claiming to be a prophet who spoke for God (Mt 26:67; Mk 14:65; Lk 22:63–65). The Roman soldiers (Mt 27:28–31; Mk 15:17–20; Jn 19:1–3) and Herod and his guards (Lk 23:11) mocked him for claiming to be a king.

Crucifixion

But Jesus' final humiliation was his crucifixion. Crucifixion was one of the most painful tortures the ancient world had

WHAT CAN YOU DO?

devised. It was so cruel that Roman citizens could not be executed this way. But it was also a powerful deterrent that the Romans often resorted to when they wanted to make a public example of those who dared to rebel against the power of Rome.

The Gospel writers did not need to describe the details of crucifixion for their audience, who were probably aware of its cruelties (Mt 27:33–56; Mk 15:22–41; Lk 23:33–49; Jn 19:17–37). It is only from the resurrection appearance of Jesus to the doubting disciple Thomas that we learn that Jesus was nailed to the cross (Jn 20:24–29).

Jesus was not the only one crucified that day. He was crucified between two criminals, who at first joined in the mockery. Some of the taunts thrown at him echoed the accusations from his trial that he would destroy the temple and that he was the Messiah-King and God's Son. "Save yourself and come down from the cross," they jeered (Mk 15:30).

The scene is eerily reminiscent of that depicted in the book of Wisdom when the wicked persecute the just one. The Jewish leaders point to Jesus' misplaced trust in God. His shameful behavior would never be rewarded by God. "He saved others; he cannot save himself. He is the King of Israel; let him come down from the cross now, and we will believe in him. He trusts in God; let God deliver him now, if he wants to; for he said, 'I am God's Son'" (Mt 27:42–43; Mk 15:29–32; Lk 23:35–38).

Crucifixion was an agonizing way to die. When the victim's arms and legs were tied or nailed to a cross, a slow process of asphyxiation began. As the muscles of the upper body grew rigid and tightened in prolonged contraction, breathing became more and more difficult and painful. The only relief was to push oneself up using one's legs. When the legs could no longer lift the body up, the victim stopped breathing and died. Death could be hastened by breaking the victim's legs (Jn 19:31–32).

Death

Jesus hung for six hours on the cross (Mk 15:25; Mt 27:45; Mk 15:33; Lk 23:44). The charge against him was written in Hebrew, Latin, and Greek and nailed above his head (Jn 19:19) so that everyone would know how the Romans dealt with anyone who claimed to be "king of the Jews."

His conduct while suffering reflected his culture's ideal. He did not cry out or whimper. His loyalty and trust of the Father never wavered despite his torture. He accepted all of this in order to fulfill the Father's plan and to give his life so that a new covenant with God would now be possible "for many" (Mk 10:45; 14:24).

Jesus' last words also reinforce his dedication to his Father. In Mark and Matthew, Jesus quotes the first lines of Psalm 22 to identify himself with the psalmist's cry of one in excruciating pain yet who trusts God completely (Mt 27:46–47;

WHAT CAN YOU DO?

Mk 15.34–35). In Luke, Jesus commits his spirit to the Father (Lk 23:46), and in John, Jesus cries out, "It is finished" (Jn 19:30).

When Jesus tells us about his Father, we distrust him. When he shows us his Home, we turn away, but when he confides in us that he is "acquainted with Grief," we listen, for that is also acquaintance of our own.

—*EMILY DICKINSON*
(1830–1886), American poet

Each Gospel writer introduces some response to Jesus' death that suggests its significance. The curtain of the temple is torn in two, signifying that Jesus' death indicated a judgment of the temple (Mt 27:51–54; Mk 15:38–39; Lk 23:45, 47). God's presence was no longer there but now could be found in the twisted body of God's suffering Son.

Matthew describes an earthquake that opens the tombs of the faithful departed, a kind of flash-forward indicating how Jesus' death would create new life for others. There is also testimony given by a Gentile centurion confirming Jesus' identity and mission as the innocent Son of God and foreshadowing the conversion of Gentiles into Jesus' kingdom community.

Only John reports Pilate's decision to break the legs of the crucified so they would not remain on the cross for the Sabbath (Jn 19:31–37). When the soldiers found Jesus already dead, they pierced his side with a spear just to make sure. And from his side flowed blood and water—his life-giving fluids that would continue to sustain the Christian community's life through baptism and Eucharist.

Burial

Because the day after the Crucifixion was both the Sabbath and the Passover, a disciple named Joseph of Arimathea, a member of the Jewish Sanhedrin (ruling council), arranged for Jesus' body to be taken down and hurriedly prepared for burial before sundown.

Only Matthew tells of the Jewish concern that Jesus' body might be stolen and a resurrection be faked (the same plot that has interested some twentieth-century skeptics and novelists!) (Mt 27:62–66). Requesting a Roman guard from Pilate, they were told to make the tomb as secure as they could—perhaps an ironic comment from a Christian viewpoint about the impossibility of stopping something that God wanted to accomplish. These guards, who would be bribed later to lie about the Resurrection, contrasted clearly with the Christian disciples who would witness to its truth.

WHAT CAN YOU DO?

THE PASSION ACCORDING TO MARK: 14:1–15:47

I. The Anointing and Last Supper

A. Plotting, Anointing, Betrayal

1. The chief priests and scribes devise their plot (14:1–2)
2. Jesus is anointed (14:3–9)
3. Judas agrees to betray Jesus (14:10–11)

B. Arrangements for the Passover Meal (14:12–16)

C. The Last Supper

1. Jesus predicts Judas's betrayal (14:17–21)
2. The Lord's Supper is instituted (14:22–25)
3. Jesus predicts Peter's denial (14:26–31)

II. Jesus' Prayer and Arrest

A. Jesus in Gethsemane (14:32–42)

B. Jesus' Arrest (14:43–52)

III. The Trials of Jesus

A. The Trial before the High Priest (14:53–65)

B. Peter's Three Denials (14:66–72)

C. The Trial before Pilate (15:1–15)

IV. The Crucifixion and Death

A. The Mockery by the Roman Soldiers (15:16–20)

B. The Crucifixion (15:21–32)

C. The Death of Jesus (15:33–41)

D. The Burial (15:42–47)

THE PASSION ACCORDING TO MATTHEW:
26:1–27:66

1. The plot to kill Jesus is devised (26:1–5)

2. Jesus is anointed at Bethany (26:6–13)

3. Judas agrees to betray Jesus (26:14–16)

4. Jesus eats the Passover meal with the disciples (26:17–25)

5. The Lord's Supper is instituted (26:26–30)

6. Peter's denial is foretold (26:31–35)

7. Jesus prays in Gethsemane (26:36–46)

8. Jesus is betrayed and arrested (26:47–56)

9. Jesus is brought before the Jewish Sanhedrin (26:57–68)

10. Peter denies Jesus (26:69–75)

11. Jesus is brought before Pilate (27:1–2)

12. Judas dies (27:3–10)

13. Jesus is questioned by Pilate (27:11–14)

14. Jesus is sentenced to death (27:15–26)

15. The Roman soldiers mock Jesus (27:27–31)

16. Jesus is crucified (27:32–44)

17. Jesus dies (27:45–56)

18. Jesus is buried (27:57–61)

19. Guards are sent to watch over the tomb (27:62–66)

WHAT CAN YOU DO?

THE PASSION ACCORDING TO LUKE: 22:1–23:56

I. The Preliminary Events

1. The leaders conspire to kill Jesus (22:1–2)
2. Judas betrays Jesus (22:3–6)
3. The disciples prepare for the Passover meal (22:7–13)
4. The Lord's Supper is instituted (22:14–20)
5. Jesus foretells his betrayal (22:21–23)
6. Jesus remarks on the disciples and their places in the kingdom (22:24–30)
7. Jesus predicts Peter's denial (22:31–34)
8. Jesus tells the disciples that a drastic change is coming (22:35–38)

II. The Passion, Death, and Burial of Jesus

1. Jesus prays on the Mount of Olives (22:39–46)
2. Jesus is arrested (22:47–53)
3. Peter denies Jesus; Jesus is brought before the council (22:54–71)
4. Jesus is delivered to Pilate; the trial begins (23:1–5)
5. Jesus is sent to Herod (23:6–12)
6. Pilate gives his judgment (23:13–16)
7. Jesus is handed over to be crucified (23:18–25)
8. Jesus travels the road to the cross (now called the Way of the Cross) (23:26–32)
9. Jesus is crucified (23:33–38)
10. The two criminals talk to Jesus (23:39–43)
11. Jesus dies (23:44–49)
12. Jesus is buried (23:50–56)

JESUS WHO SUFFERED AND DIED

THE PASSION ACCORDING TO JOHN: 18:1–19:42

I. The Arrest and Interrogation of Jesus

A. The Arrest of Jesus (18:1–11)

    1. The scene in the Garden is set (18:1–3)

    2. Jesus confronts the arresting party (18:4–9)

    3. Peter responds by striking the servant (18:10–11)

    4. Jesus is taken from the Garden to Annas (18:12–14)

B. The Interrogation of Jesus (18:15–27)

    1. Peter and the other disciple enter the high priest's palace (18:15)

    2. Peter denies Jesus the first time (18:16–18)

    3. Annas interrogates Jesus, who protests his innocence (18:19–23)

    4. Jesus is sent to Caiaphas (18:24)

    5. Peter denies Jesus the second and third times (18:25–27)

II. The Trial of Jesus before Pilate

    1. Jewish authorities ask Pilate to condemn Jesus (18:28–32)

    2. Pilate questions Jesus about his kingship (18:33–38)

    3. Pilate attempts to release Jesus the first time, but the crowd chooses Barabbas (18:38–40)

    4. The Roman soldiers scourge and mock Jesus (19:1–3)

    5. Pilate presents Jesus to the people, but "the Jews" shout for crucifixion (19:4–8)

    6. Pilate talks with Jesus about power (19:9–11)

    7. Pilate gives in to the demand for Jesus' crucifixion (19:12–16)

WHAT CAN YOU DO?

Jesus' Death, Our Death

We die as we live, so the saying goes. From a Christian viewpoint, Jesus' death was the culmination of a life lived in dedication to God his Father and to God's plan for a new community on earth. Jesus offered us an example of how to approach our death in full dedication to the God who has given us life. What then can we learn from Jesus about dying honorably today?

Jesus never sought death but accepted his death when it came. The meaning of his death emerged only within the larger context of God's plan. Jesus' life, ministry, death, and—as will be discussed in the next chapter—resurrection would change the relationship between God and people.

Lord, we do not know where you are going.
How can we know the way?

—*JOHN 14:5*

CHAPTER TWELVE

Jesus Who Rose from the Dead

The ending of a story gives meaning to all that has happened so far. So we must notice that the end of the Gospels is not Jesus' death but his resurrection. Had the Gospels ended with his death, they would not have been news, let alone "good news," for anyone.

The Gospel writers tell the story of Jesus' life in such a way that his resurrection to new life provided a way to make sense of his death as God's honorable Son. The Resurrection is the central event not only for Jesus but also for us. Jesus' life, death, and resurrection (Mk 8:31; 9:31; 10:33)—taken as one piece—become the foundation of the Christian experience, the source of our hope, and the driving force of our Christian mission.

The Fact of the Resurrection

Jesus died. Nobody—friend or foe—disputed or doubted that. He was hastily buried, and his disciples then had to wait through the long Sabbath until Sunday morning to prepare his body properly according to the usual burial customs. When Mary Magdalene and other women disciples came to the tomb bringing spices to anoint his body, they discovered that the tomb was empty and his body gone.

[The resurrection] was an event that was observed by no one, an event caused by God—indeed, an event in which the world of God intersected the world of time and space. . . . All that the historian as such can say is that something marvellous has happened here.

—*G. E. LADD*
Scripture scholar, *I Believe in the Resurrection of Jesus*

The empty tomb and the absent body stunned and perplexed the disciples. These facts cried out for meaning. Was the body stolen? Who had taken him away? For what purpose? What did all this mean?

What happened next was a complete surprise. The Jesus they had known, whom they had "heard . . . seen with our eyes . . . looked at and touched with our hands" (1 Jn 1:1), whom they knew had been crucified and buried, was suddenly alive again.

This new life, described as resurrection, was not just a restoration of one's former life. It was not a mere resuscitation from the dead. The prophets Elijah and Elisha had brought people back to this life, as had Jesus for the daughter of Jairus, the son of the widow of Nain, and Jesus' beloved friend Lazarus. Although their return from the dead left them temporarily alive, they would die again. Jesus' resurrection was a new life that would never again be subject to death. It was eternal life, permanent and undying existence in the presence of God forever.

As for what actually happened to Jesus of Nazareth in the tomb on that first Easter, there are no eyewitness accounts. The facts and events are shrouded in mystery, accessible only by faith but not by historical verification. From the viewpoint of history, we have a before (the death and burial of Jesus) and an after (the reports of the empty tomb and of his appearances). We have no account of what happened in between.

Making Sense out of beyond Sense

Thinking about the meaning of the Resurrection is the Christian struggle to make sense out of what is beyond sense—understanding something that is not part of our normal experience but is extremely important for how we choose to understand ourselves and our world in relation to God and others. The process of discovering the meaning of the Resurrection is the heart of our seeker's quest.

What is most apparent from the Resurrection accounts in the Gospels is that the event was not immediately intelligible. Finding the empty tomb left the disciples bewildered, confused, and grasping for various possible answers to account for it. The empty tomb was never a proof but a fact to be interpreted. The experiences of Christ risen were also surprising, but they left the disciples wondering and even doubting (Mt 28:17; Jn 20:25).

The Lord almost always showed Himself to me as risen . . . except at times when He showed me His wounds in order to encourage me when I was suffering tribulation.

—*TERESA OF ÁVILA*
(1515–1582), Spanish mystic and doctor of the Church

The meaning of Jesus' new life was also not self-evident. The first witnesses simply testified to the fact—he is risen!— with no attempt to grapple with the significance of his new existence. Their testimony simply invited others to accept the truth of their claim through trust.

The difficulty of accepting the good news about Jesus' resurrection on the testimony of others was at the root of the problem of the doubting disciple Thomas. Although we so often hear his story as one of demanding proof through his own personal encounter with the risen Christ, the real issue was that he refused to believe based on the word of others. Jesus said to him, "Have you believed because you have seen me? Blessed are those who have not seen and yet have come to believe" (Jn 20:29).

For them, as for us, finding the meaning of Jesus' resurrection required that it be put into some larger context. Because our human minds desire meaning and not just facts, facts alone are not intelligible. Historians seldom argue about the dates of the Civil War, for example, but write volumes about what the war meant to the people who were involved and to the country.

Facts only become significant when collected and placed within a larger perspective. But because these larger contexts, or perspectives, are manifold and freely chosen by the interpreters, various explanations can be suggested for what happened. Was the Civil War caused by slavery, greed, regional economics, political or social differences, or all of the above? Each explanation depends upon the context that is chosen to make sense of the facts.

Steps toward Interpretation: "According to the Scriptures"

The earliest sustained Christian reflection on the meaning of the Resurrection is in Paul's first letter to the Christian community in Corinth (1 Cor 15). It was written in the midfifties, some fifteen to thirty years before the Gospels were written. Paul reminded the community of the chain of witnesses

through which their faith was connected to the Jesus'
resurrection.

"I handed on to you as of first importance what I in
turn had received: that Christ died for our sins in accordance
with the scriptures, and that he was buried, and that he was
raised on the third day in accordance with the scriptures, and
that he appeared to Cephas [Peter], then to the twelve," to five
hundred other disciples and finally to Paul (1 Cor 15:3–5).

Paul's claim that all this happened "according to the
scriptures" reveals how the earliest Christians sought the
meaning of the Resurrection. Because all the earliest Christians
were Jews, the first and most obvious method of interpretation was to relate the Resurrection to their history with God.
The early Christians discovered several ways to express the
meaning of Jesus' resurrection in relation to God's plan of
salvation as it was described in the books of the Old Testament.

Passages from the Old Testament prophets and psalms
were applied to the Resurrection to amplify the minimal historical information about the events and to interpret their
significance for Christian believers. In this process, Jesus' good
news about the kingdom of God (Mt 4:23; 9:35; Mk 1:14–15;
Lk 4:43; 8:1; 16:16) became the Christian good news about
Jesus' resurrection (Acts 8:12, 35; 13:32–33; 17:18). Jesus
preached that God would enter into our world to create a
new community according to God's guidelines. Christians
preached that this new community had now begun through

WHAT CAN YOU DO?

the death and resurrection of Jesus and the outpouring of God's Holy Spirit on those who believed.

AN OVERVIEW OF THE RESURRECTION NARRATIVES IN EACH GOSPEL

Mark

1. The women visit the tomb and receive the message of the Resurrection (16:1–8)
2. Jesus makes other appearances in the later additions to Mark's original Gospel (16:9–20)

Matthew

1. Joseph of Arimathea buries Jesus as the women look on (27:57–61)
2. The chief priests and Pharisees send guards to the tomb (27:62–66)
3. The women visit the tomb, and an angel appears, frightening the guards. They set off to tell the disciples and meet Jesus on their way (28:1–10)
4. The priests and elders advise the guards to lie (28:11–15)
5. Jesus commissions the eleven disciples (28:16–20)

Luke

Easter Sunday Events (in the Gospel)

1. The women and Peter arrive at the empty tomb (23:56–24:12)
2. The two disciples encounter Jesus on the road to Emmaus (24:13–35)

3. Jesus appears to the disciples in Jerusalem (24:36–43)

4. esus commissions the disciples (24:44–49)

5. Jesus ascends into heaven (24:50–53)

Other Appearances during the Forty Days (in Acts of the Apostles)

1. Jesus instructs the eleven apostles (Acts 1:1–8)

2. Jesus ascends into heaven (Acts 1:9–11)

John

Chapter 20: The Risen Christ as a Catalyst for Faith

1. Simon Peter and the Beloved Disciple find the tomb empty (20:1–10)

2. Jesus appears to Mary Magdalene (20:11–18)

3. Jesus appears to the disciples (20:19–23)

4. Jesus appears to Thomas (20:24–29)

5. The conclusion is given (20:30–31)

Chapter 21: Pastoral Directives for the Community

1. Jesus appears at the seaside; the disciples make an unusual catch of fish (21:1–8)

2. Jesus and the disciples eat a meal of bread and fish (21:9–14)

3. Jesus asks Simon Peter three times if he loves him (21:15–19)

4. Jesus talks of the Beloved Disciple (21:20–25)

The Resurrection as God's Act

In exploring the meaning of the Resurrection, we must ask two questions: How did it happen? and Why did it happen?

WHAT CAN YOU DO?

For the early Christians, how the Resurrection happened was, as we say today, a no-brainer. The earliest apostolic preaching identified the Resurrection as a divine deed of power and specified that God raised Jesus from the dead (Acts 2:24, 32; 3:15, 26; 4:10; 10:40; 13:30, 37; Rom 10:9; 1 Cor 6:14).

In order for something so marvelous and extraordinary to occur, God, the origin and giver of all life, obviously had to do it. Their thinking would have been similar to that described earlier in chapter 10 concerning the explanation of Jesus' signs and wonders. The Resurrection was the sign of the salvation that God had promised long ago. It was also the sign that Jesus had promised as the confirmation of his mission (Mt 12:40).

Why the Resurrection happened was a much more complicated question. First of all, little direct help could be gleaned from the Scriptures because Jewish belief before Jesus' time did not include any consistent teaching about life after death. The general view could be summed up by the pessimistic wisdom teacher called Ecclesiastes, who taught that "the living know that they will die, but the dead know nothing; they have no more reward, and even the memory of them is lost" (Eccl 9:5).

But this belief seemed to lose its grip on Judaism beginning in the second century before Christ. We do not have a clear idea of how or when the idea of resurrection originated in Judaism, but we find hints of it in the second book of Maccabees and the book of Wisdom, which date from this period. Although the Sadducee group continued to deny the Resurrection (Mt 22:23; Mk 12:18; Lk 20:27), the Pharisees, whose teachings Paul the Apostle embraced from his youth, apparently held some type of belief in a resurrection (Acts 23:6–8).

Because the Resurrection was something only God could do and because actions reveal one's character, clues about the meaning of the Resurrection could be taken from what scripture said about God's character. The Resurrection revealed God's love and indicated how God's power was enlisted to bring about a new creation.

The Resurrection as a Revelation of God's Character

When God appeared to Moses on Sinai to seal the covenant, God offered a capsule summary of God's own character. "The LORD passed before him, and proclaimed, 'The LORD, the LORD, a God merciful and gracious, slow to anger, and abounding in steadfast love and faithfulness, keeping steadfast love for the thousandth generation, forgiving iniquity and transgression and sin, yet by no means clearing the guilty, but visiting the iniquity of the parents upon the children and the children's children, to the third and the fourth generation' " (Ex 34:6–7).

This self-description highlights the special type of covenant love that God exhibits. In Jesus' world, love was identified as group attachment (communion) through group bonding (a commitment of faith or trust), with or without the romantic stress on feelings of affection so necessary today. The most desirable characteristics of love were an absolute loyalty and an exclusive attachment.

Christ is arisen.
Joy to thee, mortal!
Empty His prison,
Broken its portal!

—J. W. VON GOETHE
(1749–1832), German poet and dramatist

God's steadfast or loyal love, the divine attachment to the Jewish people sealed with a covenant commitment, was distinctive in its constancy. Though the people might waver in their loyalty and attachment, God did not. "Know therefore that the Lord your God is God, the faithful God who maintains covenant loyalty with those who love him and keep his commandments, to a thousand generations" (Dt 7:9).

God's steadfast love would encourage the community to seek God first as its generous (merciful) patron who would protect them and provide for their needs. The people could be confident that God would do this because of the constant evidence from their history that God had always rescued them when they were in a difficult situation. The bond of their relationship gave them confidence that God would use the divine power to fulfill God's side of the covenant relationship.

But what if God's commitment to those who had been completely faithful to the covenant, in particular those who gave their life because of this loyalty, did not simply end with their death? What would happen if God chose for the covenant to continue beyond death?

The second book of Maccabees suggests such a situation. Seven brothers and their mother were arrested during the Jewish rebellion against their Greek overlords. They were forced to eat pork, which was forbidden by their religious food laws. Each one resisted, was brutally tortured, and died a martyr for the covenant beliefs. The second brother, "when he was at his last breath, he said [to the king], 'You accursed wretch, you dismiss us from this present life, but the King of the universe will raise us up to an everlasting renewal of life, because we have died for his laws' " (2 Mc 7:9).

Faith seeks the earthly Jesus not as a dead teacher, but as the living Lord, whose word and work were not merely accomplished once upon a time, but are now made ever present in the community.

—*REGINALD H. FULLER*
Scripture scholar, *The Formation of the Resurrection Narratives*

Finally, after watching her seven sons die, the mother cried out, "I do not know how you came into being in my womb. It was not I who gave you life and breath, nor I who set in order the elements within each of you. Therefore the Creator of the world, who shaped the beginning of human-kind and devised the origin of all things, will in his mercy give life and breath back to you again, since you now forget yourselves for the sake of his laws" (2 Mc 7:22–23).

Because Jesus also died in fidelity to God and the new covenant with the kingdom community, Jesus' resurrection to new life could be viewed as God's reward for his martyr-dom. Motivated by steadfast love, God restored Jesus to a new life that will never end.

The Resurrection as Part of God's Plan

As we have noted, the Bible recounts the stories of God's desire for a relationship with all humanity, with Abraham and his descendants, with Jesus, and with his kingdom com-munity. Because the history of our world is also a history of these divine relationships, it is a "salvation" history. Before *salvation* became a theological term, it simply meant rescuing someone from a difficult situation. It was the duty of the head of the household. Consequently God, the head of the household of faith, would be expected to act when the covenant people required rescue.

The final rescue, of course, would be from the hold of death, which the ancients understood as the final triumph of sinfulness. Everything exists through God's creative power. As the creation account in Genesis makes clear, human beings receive life through God's Spirit (Gn 2:7; Jb 33:4).

But the breath of life is temporary, and from the moment of birth the forces of evil begin their assault on the person. As evil encroaches more and more, sickness and sin disrupt the right order of the body and the person's relationships with others and God until the result is death. Death was the termination of one's relationship with this world and with God.

But suppose God's power to give life was yoked to God's desire for a relationship. God's love would conquer the stranglehold of death, and God's ultimate rescue would snatch us from death. God's ultimate gift would be eternal life.

In fact, this ultimate rescue is hinted at by the prophet Hosea who declared, "Come, let us return to the Lord; for it is he who has torn, and he will heal us; he has struck down, and he will bind us up. After two days he will revive us; on the third day he will raise us up, that we may live before him" (Hos 6:1–2). This revival would occur because those who had been faithful had lived as God desired: "For I desire steadfast love and not sacrifice, the knowledge of God rather than burnt offerings" (Hos 6:6). This was the basis of the mercy agenda that Jesus taught as the kingdom way.

As God's beloved Son, Jesus had lived out perfectly the relation of the Son to the Father. The Resurrection, then, could be thought of as the reward to Jesus for his dedication

WHAT CAN YOU DO?

to the kingdom relationship. Thus God, the Creator of all things, was recognized as the one who also gives new life to the dead through resurrection. Paul, in fact, reads this kind of faith back to the time of Abraham and indicated that this doubly life-giving God was actually the one "in whom he [Abraham] believed, who gives life to the dead and calls into existence the things that do not exist" (Rom 4:17).

Resurrection is God's action, motivated by love, because God does not want the relationship built up over the course of a life to end in death. Rather, through God's power, one is gifted with new life (a new creation) beyond death. This new life and relationship with the God who gives life are therefore deathless or eternal.

The Resurrection as a Revision of Belief

Once Christians recognized that the Resurrection was God's final saving act of love and that it was the triumph of God's desire for communion over evil's desire for disorder, they were able to revise their understanding of Jesus' life and especially his death, which at the time had made no sense to them.

To revise means to see anew. We revise a book, for example, when there is new information that needs to be taken into account, a new situation in which the book will be read, or a new perspective that offers a fresh way of interpreting things. The Resurrection offered Christians all of these.

Jesus' resurrection was an event signaling the end of the old situation in which death was the end not only of life but also of one's relationship with God. The Resurrection also offered a new situation in which the importance of one's relationship with God before death became the critical factor in determining one's future after death. The Resurrection also provided a new lens through which the followers of Jesus could see what the ministry and passion of Jesus had really been about.

Caesar was more talked about in his time than Jesus, Plato taught more science than Christ. People still discuss the Roman ruler and the Greek philosopher, but who nowadays is hotly for Caesar or against him; and who now are the Platonists and the anti-Platonists? There are still people who love Him and who hate Him. . . . The fury of so many against Him is a proof that He is not dead.

—*GIOVANNI PAPINI*
Italian journalist and writer

How could such a good son, "Jesus of Nazareth, a man attested to you by God with deeds of power, wonders, and signs that God did through him among you, as you yourselves know," be crucified and killed? The Resurrection revealed that it was possible only "according to the definite plan and foreknowledge of God" (Acts 2:22–23).

But there were no examples of a suffering messiah in the Scriptures, no models that could shed light on the surprising connection between Christ's suffering and glory. So the Christian scribes began to gather clues from various sources to put together a coherent explanation for God's gift of new life to Jesus. Their search led them to realize that Jesus' resurrection was not accidental but, like his death, was directly connected to his loyal service to God's kingdom. The Resurrection was the reward of the Father for the behavior of Jesus as an honorable Son.

The Resurrection as the Reward of the Righteous

When describing the reward that one reaped from good deeds, Jesus said that "whoever welcomes a prophet in the name of a prophet will receive a prophet's reward; and whoever welcomes a righteous person in the name of a righteous person will receive the reward of the righteous" (Mt 10:41).

Righteous here describes a person who has lived up to all the demands of a relationship. But what is the reward of the righteous? It is God's gift of new life for the "steadfast love" that the person has exhibited by living out the demands of the covenant.

In an interesting passage from the wisdom of Sirach, the common biblical assumption that God will certainly "reward individuals according to their conduct" is linked with the idea that "when you come to serve the Lord, prepare yourself for testing" (Sir 2:2). Those who are "steadfast" and "do not depart," who are tested "in the furnace of humiliation," who "trust in him," "fear the Lord, wait for his mercy; [and] do not stray" will not lose their reward. "Has anyone trusted in the Lord and been disappointed? Or has anyone persevered in the fear of the Lord and been forsaken? Or has anyone called upon him and been neglected? For the Lord is compassionate and merciful; he forgives sins and saves in time of distress" (Sir 2:10–11).

The Scriptures reveal several examples of persons who choose righteousness, persevere in their loyalty to God despite persecution and suffering, and so deserve the reward God has promised.

The Innocent Righteous One

In the Old Testament there are several instances of innocent persons who are persecuted and endangered but who are vindicated by God's intervention. Job, for example, lost everything because Satan, or the tempter, wanted to show God how fickle Job's loyalty really was. Job persevered and refused to acknowledge any wrongdoing. In the end, God rewarded Job with even more than he had originally lost.

Daniel and his companions were persecuted in exile because of their loyalty to their God and the regulations of the Jewish law. When they were thrown into a fiery furnace and later into a lions' den, God intervened to rescue them for their fidelity. God also used the perceptive Daniel to save the beautiful and God-fearing Susanna from her false accusers.

In examining Jesus' passion in the previous chapter, we alluded to the persecution of the innocent righteous Son of God (Wis 2:10–24). The author of Wisdom also suggests how God will take care of him. Because "God created us for incorruption, and made us in the image of his own eternity" (Wis 2:23), "the souls of the righteous are in the hand of God," and so "they will receive great good, because God tested them and found them worthy of himself; like gold in the furnace he tried them, and like a sacrificial burnt offering he accepted them" (Wis 3:1–6). Through their suffering they were rewarded with a deathless fellowship with God.

The Martyred Prophet

The prophets provide another image of the righteous who suffer on behalf of their dedication to God. Their dedication to speaking God's word, especially when it proclaimed judgment and the demand for conversion, often provoked resistance, ridicule, and rejection by kings, priests, and even other prophets. God always rewarded the loyalty of the prophets, providing for their needs and protecting them from harm.

By the time of Jesus, the suffering prophet was common-place. Jesus refused to flee from Herod's death threat because "it is impossible for a prophet to be killed outside of Jerusalem."

At the same time Jesus also stereotyped Jerusalem as "the city that kills the prophets and stones those who are sent to it" (Lk 13:33–34).

Jesus also linked the prophets' suffering to the long, sad history of innocent murder victims in the Bible. "Therefore I send you prophets, sages, and scribes, some of whom you will kill and crucify, and some you will flog in your synagogues and pursue from town to town, so that upon you may come all the righteous blood shed on earth, from the blood of righteous Abel to the blood of Zechariah son of Barachiah, whom you murdered between the sanctuary and the altar" (Mt 23:34–35). The reference was to the first and last murders mentioned in the Hebrew Bible (Abel in Genesis 4:1–16 and the prophet Zechariah in 2 Chronicles 24:20–22, which is the last book in the Hebrew arrangement of the Bible).

The Suffering Servant (Son)

Perhaps no passages were as important for configuring a new understanding of a suffering messiah than the four servant songs found in the prophet Isaiah (Is 42:1–4; 49:1–6; 50:4–9; 52:13–53:12). The Jews never associated this mysterious figure with any messianic hope as the Christians did. For the Jews this mysterious suffering servant was more likely an unnamed prophet or perhaps even a symbol of the chosen people. Christians never would have been so attracted to these texts had it not been for the demand to explain the suffering of Jesus as the Messiah.

These four songs summarize the whole career of the servant (or child/son as the Greek word could also mean). In the first, God described the call and commission of the servant to bring forth justice in the whole earth. In the second, the servant described his appointment by God, his abilities, and the difficulties of his mission to gather Israel and be a light for the whole earth. In the third, the servant described his teaching mission, the opposition it generated, and how with God's help he would succeed. Finally, the servant, though innocent and righteous, suffered and died and was buried. But his death had some vicarious merit for many others. So he was vindicated by God and promised "a portion with the great" (Is 53:12) after his death.

The truth is, it is not Jesus as historically known, but Jesus as spiritually arisen within men, that is significant for our time, and can help it.

—ALBERT SCHWEITZER
(1875–1965), German theologian,
physician, and missionary, *The Quest for the Historical Jesus*

By identifying Jesus the Messiah as this suffering servant/son, Christians found the way to connect Jesus' suffering and death with his resurrection. His suffering service to God's justice was rewarded. His resurrection and placement at God's right hand were the fulfillment of God's promised reward for his righteous behavior.

The suffering servant also clarified how Jesus' death could help others to achieve the righting of wrongly ordered relationships and overcome the effects of sin. His resurrection was the first step in bringing humanity into right relationship with God. Thus anyone who connected himself or herself to Jesus' death and resurrection through faith and commitment to Jesus and his way of life would also share the reward of eternal life with God.

Once Christians formulated their new description of the Messiah as the suffering servant/martyred prophet/innocent righteous one, then Jesus' death could be understood as a sign of his complete offering of himself in service. It was a form of sacrifice in which the death of the victim signified that the offering was complete and nothing could be taken back. As Christian ideas about the significance of Jesus' death and resurrection took shape over the next century, these various descriptions played an important role.

The Resurrection Stories: God's Reward for the Honorable Son

The Resurrection accounts in the Gospels were shaped by the same process that guided how the rest of the stories about Jesus were written. These written versions of the Resurrection events depended upon the oral reports of the disciples that were rooted in the historical events of that first Easter morning. And like the Gospel accounts of Jesus' life and death, these Resurrection stories were "invented" (in the ancient rhetorical sense of finding suitable arguments) by the writers to demonstrate that the Resurrection was God's response to the life and death of Jesus, God's honorable Servant/Son.

The Gospel writers presented arguments to persuade their audience that new life was the reward for the Son's fidelity and loyalty to the Father. Understood in the larger context of God's plan for salvation, Christians could see how it was "necessary that the Messiah should suffer these things and then enter into his glory" (Lk 24:26). The Gospel writers' recognition that Jesus' death was a necessity came after the Resurrection; they didn't understand Jesus' death in this way while he was dying or before he rose from the dead.

The Gospel writers' primary interest was theological (to tell about God and how humanity could be in relationship with God through Jesus). They told about what God—the creator and giver of life—motivated by love, was willing and able and adamant about doing for Jesus and for all of God's "servants" who live in right relationship despite hardships, temptations, and sufferings. They depict the kingdom way leading to eternal life but through suffering, and they remind us that Jesus' passage to the Father will someday be ours.

The Gospel writers' second interest was to deepen people's commitment and conversion to Christ and to establish their involvement in the Christian community. They suggested that what happened to Christ as this suffering servant/child was a preview of what will happen to all his followers who imitate his example.

Jesus' tasks as prophet, priest, and king were fulfilled in the Resurrection. The suffering prophet reaped a prophet's reward. The reconciling priest brought about people's escape from evil and their entrance into a new communion with God. The wise and powerful king established a new community of justice for all humanity.

Christ's Resurrection: Sign of God's Presence and Power

The belief that Jesus was risen to new life and had appeared to the disciples was shared by all the early Christians. The Gospel writers described the appearances of the risen Christ in revelatory terms. During these Resurrection appearances, the risen Christ also gave to his followers a share in God's power (the Holy Spirit) so that they could continue his work.

The disciples encountered the living Lord, who appeared or "allowed himself to be seen" (Greek, *opthe*). The writers stressed Jesus' free self-disclosure during the Resurrection experiences. The risen Christ allowed himself to be discovered under forms that we can recognize: in his own body, as a gardener, as a stranger who accompanies us on our journey,

WHAT CAN YOU DO?

as a table companion, and as the bread and wine that became part of Christian worship.

Many New Testament authors stressed Christ's abiding presence. Matthew described Jesus as "Emmanuel, which means 'God is with us'" (1:23) and reminded us that "where two or three are gathered in my name, I am there among them" (18:20). He also reported Jesus' final words as a promise of continued presence: "And remember, I am with you always, to the end of the age" (28:20).

Luke illustrated the hidden presence of the risen Christ on the Easter journey of the two disciples to Emmaus (Lk 24:13–35). Even though Jesus accompanied them as a mysterious stranger who opened their minds and hearts to God's presence by interpreting Scripture, they did not recognize him until "the breaking of the bread" in a fellowship meal. Through word and sacrament, and as companion on our life journey, Jesus revealed his abiding presence in our community.

Christ . . . does not really teach one anything, but by being brought into his presence one becomes something. And everybody is predestined to his presence. Once at least in his life each man walks with Christ to Emmaus.

—*OSCAR WILDE*
(1854–1900), Irish poet and dramatist, *De Profundis*

John, too, described the abiding presence of Christ through the Holy Spirit, or Paraclete. Though Jesus had departed bodily so that God's plan for humanity could continue, he sent the Spirit to continue his work. "The Advocate, the Holy Spirit, whom the Father will send in my name, will teach you everything, and remind you of all that I have said to you" (Jn 14:26).

The risen Christ, when he shows himself to his friends, takes on the countenance of all races and each can hear him in his own tongue.

—*HENRI DE LUBAC*
(1896–1991), French Jesuit theologian, *Catholicism*

Paul recognized this special experience of Christ's presence as the fundamental characteristic of the Christian community. He described the unified diversity of the Christian community by analogy with the human body: "We, who are many, are one body in Christ, and individually we are members one of another" (Rom 12:5; 1 Cor 10:17; 12:12–27).

For Paul, this embodiment was not merely something spiritual but more like a physical locale in which Christians existed. "For in the one Spirit we were all baptized into one body—Jews or Greeks, slaves or free—and we were all made to drink of one Spirit" (1 Cor 12:13).

Paul's code term for this new Christian reality was *living in Christ.* This was the mental framework behind his famous declaration that "for in Christ Jesus you are all children of God through faith. As many of you as were baptized into Christ have clothed yourselves with Christ. There is no longer

WHAT CAN YOU DO?

Jew or Greek, there is no longer slave or free, there is no longer male and female; for all of you are one in Christ Jesus" (Gal 3:26–28). Paul certainly knew that these human sources of domination and devaluation continued to exist. His point was that in the Christian community they were no longer applicable.

In the book of Revelation, John's four visions of Christ's presence echoed the common chorus of New Testament witnesses. John's visions revealed that the distinctive Christian identity was rooted in the awareness that reality was filled with the hidden presence of Christ. To know who we are as Christians demanded an acknowledgment that hidden beneath the social structures of our community lurks the mysterious presence of Christ himself and that of his Holy Spirit. Thus the Christian community itself becomes a revelation—a picture for the world of Christ's hidden presence.

Christ's Resurrection as the Source of Our Hope

Jesus' resurrection, God's reward for the honorable Son/ Servant who remains loyal and steadfast through his suffering, becomes the lens through which his life and death finally become clear. His sonships, his aims, tasks, and strategies were part of a relationship that Jesus established with God while here on earth.

This relationship of Father to Son continued not because Jesus wanted it to continue but because God did. When God, the giver of life, gave new life to Jesus, death took on a new meaning. Death ends only our earthly life, not our relationship with God. The fidelity and love established and intensified during life does not end with death. God offered Jesus a new life, a new and continuing relationship that would never end.

This gift was an important demonstration and pledge of God's faithfulness. Once again God intervened in history to maintain the relationship with Jesus. What God did for Jesus in the middle of history, God will do for us at the end of our history. The condition, of course, is that we establish and maintain a relationship to God that follows Jesus' example. Our covenant relationship will not end with our death, but continue through and beyond death.

Christ's Resurrection as the Inspiration of Christian Mission

The Resurrection narratives illustrate the relationship between the risen Christ and the community of disciples. The disciples in these accounts also serve as examples for those who decide to follow Jesus and his teachings. Like the first disciples, today's believers live between the experience of the Resurrection and the expectation that the Son of man will return in glory at the end of time (Mt 24:29–31; Mk 13:24–26; Lk 21:25–28). The person today who follows Jesus of Nazareth is also called to continue the mission and ministry that Jesus began.

As we study these stories of Jesus, we discover the basic pattern that guides Christian discipleship. The disciples moved from an experience of the risen Christ to an understanding of its meaning and then to a response that expressed this meaning in the actions of their everyday lives.

Experiencing the Risen One

Every Christian is a Christian because, in some way or other, he or she has experienced the risen Christ. As the various Resurrection narratives indicate, some experience Christ in a special bodily form. Others experience him through the words and lives of others. Still others experience him in the sharing of a meal. This experience of the risen Christ is always the essential starting point of Christian belief.

The Resurrection stories also reveal how hard it is to detect the Risen One. The disciples on their way to Emmaus failed to recognize Jesus as he shared their journey and only recognized him at their meal in the breaking of the bread. Again when Jesus appeared to all the gathered disciples on Easter evening, they were alarmed and thought he was a ghost.

Experience Demands Understanding

The experience of the risen Christ as alive and active in our lives demands an interpretation. The fact of the Resurrection needs to be understood in order for the meaning or significance of it to make a difference to us. Unless we discover its meaning, the Resurrection remains simply a fact without any relevance for our lives.

But by using the Old Testament passages about the Messiah, in particular how he had to suffer and be rewarded as part of God's own plan for bringing about the forgiveness of sin and the beginning of a new kingdom way of life, Christians discover and recognize the plan of God working in their lives. Reading and studying the Scriptures does not simply give us an experience of the risen Christ. Scripture reading gives us clues about how God has broken into our world in the past and how we might expect God to do it again. Without the guidance of Scripture, it can be extremely difficult to detect the presence and activity of God at work in our world.

Understanding Leads to Action

The Resurrection stories demonstrate that our Christian lives never stop when we have understood the significance of our experience of the risen Christ. Curiously enough, whenever we try to hold on to Christ and bask in the enjoyment of his presence, he reminds us that we must go forth and become witnesses to what we have experienced.

The disciples journeying to Emmaus discovered this. After their heartwarming conversation with the mysterious stranger, they finally recognized his identity in the breaking of the bread. Then, suddenly, "he vanished from their sight" (Lk 24:31). Despite their astonishment, they immediately set out to share their experience with the other disciples, only to find that Christ had already appeared to them too.

The Lord's Resurrection is not an isolated fact, it is a fact that concerns the whole of mankind; from Christ it extends to the world; it has a cosmic importance . . . the source of meaning of the human drama, the solution of the problem of evil, the origin of a new form of life, to which we give the name of Christianity.

—*POPE PAUL VI*
Easter Sermon, 1964

The pattern is clear. When they understood their experience of the risen Christ, announcing this Good News—evangelization—began. Good news is always for sharing. When the experience of the risen Christ becomes a reality in us and our community, no one has to tell us to share it. As individuals, we are so filled with Christ that we take on his mind and heart. We begin to see the world the way he did and act in it as he would. We become the presence of Christ to our world. Evangelization starts with our own example.

As St. Francis of Assisi was reported to have said, "We must preach with our lives, and use words if we have to."

Evangelization begins when we are changed by our contact with the risen Christ. The mystery of the Resurrection is that Christ transforms us into himself through the power of the Holy Spirit. As individuals, we become Christs for others. Our lives become the gospel that people can most easily read. As individuals and communities, we become the body of Christ, to be taken, blessed, broken, and shared so that a world might live.

PART 3

For the Seeker Going Further

Do you *also want to become his disciples?*

— *JOHN 9:27*

CHAPTER THIRTEEN

Following Christ Today

The Jesus who offered himself as the teacher for those first two seekers still offers himself as our teacher today. His original invitation is now extended to us: "Come and see." Come to be in a personal relationship with him and see the world anew. This relationship opens up a passage that leads through death to new life with God forever.

For those first seekers who chose to become Jesus' disciples, following meant not just the acceptance of some abstract teaching but also the identification with the teacher in an everyday personal relationship. When Jesus chose the twelve disciples that he wanted as the symbolic foundation of his kingdom community, Mark noted that the first requirement was that they "be with him" before they are "sent out to proclaim the message, and to have authority to cast out demons" (Mk 3:14–15). Communion precedes proclamation and the reordering of life.

Christian discipleship is portrayed not only as the acceptance of a master's teaching, but as the identification of oneself with the master's way of life and destiny in an intimate, personal following of him.

—*JOSEPH A. FITZMYER, S.J.*
Scripture scholar, *The Gospel According to Luke*

Following Jesus

Following Jesus has a double connotation. It may be understood as imitation (following his example) or as sharing a journey (following in his footsteps). In either case, following Jesus opens up a new way of relating to God and to others. We discover this new kingdom way of living not only in the particular events of Jesus' ministry (his parables, meals, and miracles) and in his suffering and death but also in the whole pattern that emerges from the gospel story.

Christian discipleship is the way we live out our relationship with God and with others in the Christian community. Our spiritual lives as *Christ-ians* are patterned after the example of Jesus, the *Christ*. We strive to become like Jesus. As Paul described it, we put on the mind of Christ (Phil 2:5) and then are able to speak and act as he did. Our discipleship—following Jesus—is a relationship that is based on seeing as he did and being the kind of person he was.

When Jesus invites us to come and be with him, he is inviting us to be his companions. This relationship has five stages. In response to our **call** into a relationship with him and our **commitment** to him and to this relationship, we assume with him the **co-mission** of building the kingdom community. This will demand the lifelong process of **conversion,** through which we take on his vision of reality, his values, his goals, and his roles in service to God's transforming presence in our midst. Because of the total investment of ourselves in this relationship, there will always be a **cost** resulting from our involvement.

The Call

Christian discipleship always begins with an *experience of God* (a divine self-revelation) through Jesus. God always takes the initiative in relating to us. Our discipleship begins with a word from Jesus, a personal call that is our "vocation." Jesus' invitation to "follow me!" demands our personal response (see Mt 4:18–22; Mk 1:16–20; Lk 5:1–11; Jn 1:35–51). Discipleship continues as our expression of life as lived in response to this divine call.

The Commitment

Unless we have established a true bond with God, there can be no discipleship. This involves first of all that we accept with trust (faith) the gift of the one who calls and invites us into relationship. Second, we entrust ourselves to this mysterious other. Our commitment is not only to the other person but also to the relationship itself. We strive to do all that is necessary to keep this bond intact, to nurture and strengthen it and make it thrive.

The Co-mission

We live out our relationship with God by participating in the mission of Jesus. That mission is to create a community of disciples who are in right relationship with God and with one another. When we do this, we realize the dream of God for a community of justice, love, and peace. Through our co-mission we carry on Jesus' earthly ministry by sharing his roles for bringing about God's kingdom:

- **the prophetic task:** to witness both in words and in deeds, to announce the good news of God's mysterious saving presence among us for the transformation of all reality

- **the priestly task:** to infuse all our actions and all the situations of our daily lives with the sanctifying presence of God

- **the kingly task:** to order all things and all activities according to Jesus' vision and values and so bring about the dream of God for a kingdom community

The Conversion

Conversion (Greek, *metanoia,* "to change one's mind, outlook or attitude"; Latin, *convertere,* "to turn back around, or go in another direction") is a conscious decision to live more responsibly in the light of our faith relationship. Conversion is a complex and dynamic process of re-forming one's life by turning toward God and away from the evil forces that affect the systems of this world. It is a lifelong challenge to order ourselves and our world according to the vision and values of Jesus' worldview and live out the obligations (Latin, *ob-ligare,* what is done "on account of the bond") of the new relationship in the community of disciples. The process of conversion follows three general phases.

- **Information:** To follow Jesus, we must learn how he sees the world, how he understands its workings, and how he evaluates it in relation to God's mysterious presence working for salvation, that is, the right relationship of all reality to God. As the expression of God's creative and self-revealing word to us, the Bible is a special and privileged source for discovering clues about who God is, how God is present, and how God is working to create a kingdom community in the world. The Bible also gives us cues about how we are to act in response to God's mysterious presence. The Bible helps us know the mysterious other in our relationship.

- **Conformation:** Simply knowing about Jesus is never enough. We must take the information we acquire and make sense of it and integrate it into our lives. Becoming a Christian means adopting a new way of seeing and of being. Jesus' vision and values must become our own.

- **Transformation:** The phases of information and conformation are incomplete unless these interior changes are translated into action and changed behavior. Our lives gain new meaning because of our relationship with God, with Jesus, and with the community of disciples who are most appropriately described as "friends" (Jn 15:15). This new meaning enables us to actually live differently from how we lived before we knew Jesus.

The Cost

Living out our relationship with God and others will always cost us. Being disciples means paying this price to be like Jesus and carry on his work in our world. Putting on the mind of Christ changes everything about our outlook, our values, and our behavior. Joining with others who share Jesus' vision and values will bring us into tension with the commonly accepted vision and values of our culture.

Jesus spent his time saving the world with a simple yet radical message. He gathered people who were willing to start living in relationships that were grounded in love, expressed in justice, and oriented to the fullness of life for all. This kind of living is in opposition to the ever present greed and quest for power that cause so much suffering across the globe. Christians (and others who have made similar choices of lifestyle) will continue to pay for their commitment to kingdom values and behavior. Sometimes the price is subtle, but sometimes a Christian's commitment to kingdom living can lead to loss of friends, job, home, or even life.

> It costs so much to be a full human being that there are very few who have the enlightenment or the courage, to pay the price. . . . One has to abandon altogether the search for security, and reach out to the risk of living with both arms. One has to embrace the world like a lover. One has to accept pain as a condition of existence. One has to court doubt and darkness as the cost of knowing. One needs a will stubborn in conflict, but apt always to total acceptance of every consequence of living and dying.
>
> —*MORRIS L. WEST*
> novelist, *The Shoes of the Fisherman*

Following the Way of Lifelong Conversion

Jesus invites us not only to come and be with him but to see the world as he does and so be in the world in the same way he is. At the core of Jesus the Teacher's agenda was the delineation of the new kingdom worldview that shifted everything for those who accepted it.

However, this Good News about God's kingdom is a threat to the way we already view the world. What if things are not as we think they are? What if things could be different? What would our world be like if God were recognized as its real and final authority?

These what-if questions can propel us into new realities. We cross the borders of our familiar world and enter a new creation—a world where the mystery and power of God are always and everywhere at work transforming our ordinary life into an extraordinary experience.

Adopting a new worldview was not so easy when Jesus called his first disciples. The worldview in which these disciples had grown up—one supported and reinforced by their culture—produced a rigid and closed system of thought. This made it difficult to adjust to new teaching. Not only did Jesus' followers have to cope with new information, they had to integrate it into a system of thought that made no room for new information. But when they did finally see themselves as "friends" of Jesus and as adopted children of their heavenly King and Patron, the Father of Jesus the Christ, they began to be transformed from Jews into Christians.

As therapists know so well, a revised self-image is perhaps the most important single factor in human change. Seeing oneself differently always leads to new ways of behaving. Changing our perspective through the assent and adoption of the world as Jesus envisions it will demand realigning the components of our whole being in such a way that we will continue to experience the world but with God as its center. This unordinary way is, in fact, so extraordinary that it brings about a total transformation of our lives.

A billion men have since professed his [Christ's] way and never followed it.

—*THOMAS WOLFE*
(1900–1938), American writer

Since the adoption of this kingdom worldview has consequences for every dimension of life, committing ourselves to it and then living out the responsibilities of this commitment can be very frightening. This challenge was perhaps even more frightening to Jesus' original audience, for whom change was not a positive value. In their world, which did not experience today's constant and dizzying pace of global technology and social change, any change was looked upon with suspicion and even fear.

And it's not enough to simply accept the truth of a new worldview. True conversion begins with acceptance but must continue to change in our values and actions. Becoming a Christian disciple demands more than just "knowing the catechism." It requires putting on a whole new way of life. There are several different aspects of whole-life conversion.

Affective conversion demands that we take responsibility for our emotional health and development. We change

FOLLOWING CHRIST TODAY

our accepted habits of feeling and intuitions. We must overcome the dysfunctions introduced by our previous emotional attitudes. We must reorganize our sensitivity, for example, to those who are suffering, oppressed, marginalized, or devalued in any way, according to Christ's example. We must constantly discover ways to purge our emotions of anger and other destructive, aggressive, and violent behaviors.

Rational conversion demands that we take responsibility for the truth or falsity, the adequacy or inadequacy of our convictions and their explanation. Because divine mysteries are revealed to us, we must constantly grope for more understandable descriptions of these mysteries even though we know our human knowledge will never adequately explain them. We can never think deeply or thoroughly enough about the mystery of God and God's presence in our lives.

Moral conversion demands that we take responsibility for the correctness of our judgments and for the formation of our conscience. Identifying God as the center of our world shifts everything else in our value system. If we see the world as Jesus does, we come to value it as he does. We discover such kingdom values as nondomination, justice, inclusiveness, and service. It takes a lifetime of commitment to put those values into action. And knowing what is right is no guarantee that we will do what is right. Living a God-centered life is a continual challenge.

Religious conversion demands that we take responsibility for our response to God's self-revelation. Not only must we change our ideas about God, but we must also change our responses to God in prayer and in our lives. As Christians we adopt a distinctive understanding of God as a trinity of persons in relation to one another and to us. When we live in light of a God-dominated reality, everything we do becomes a pursuit of God's presence and an endeavor to learn how to relate to that mystery.

Social conversion demands that we take responsibility for the structure and functioning of our communities. Our commitment to right relationships will bring us into conflict with the present systems that define our worlds and regulate our lives. Our lives as Christians now inaugurate the kingdom of God not only in our individual lives but also in our families, our faith communities, our societies, and our global systems.

As Christians, our challenge is to refashion our world in the image of Jesus' dream of the kingdom of God. When we adopt Jesus' kingdom worldview and live it out consistently, domination becomes service, sovereignty becomes compassion, weakness becomes strength, foolishness becomes wisdom, suffering becomes hope, vulnerability becomes power, and death becomes life.

Discovering our new identity as Christian disciples changes everything. When we can let go of our old familiar worldview and live in this new reality that finds God's transcendent presence everywhere, life is forever changed.

Five Important Things to Remember about Jesus

As you come to the end of this *Seeker's Guide,* there are certain essentials you need to grasp and remember. Over the centuries, scholars, teachers, and ecclesial organizations have formulated a lot of theology about Jesus. Some of their works are listed at the end of this book. But these five aspects of Jesus' identity and purpose are at the foundation of Christian experience everywhere.

1. Jesus Is Nothing without God

Sometimes it is difficult to avoid Christolatry—idolizing Jesus by putting so much emphasis on him that we forget that he exists only as part of a much wider and more mysterious reality that we call God. He recognized this by his understanding of himself as a son. A son does not generate himself but exists only because of the life-giving power of a father. Jesus' existence on earth, his mission, his teaching, miracles, and meals also occurred as part of a larger plan for reconciling all humanity with God (2 Cor 5:16–21).

We often approach Jesus the Teacher and want him to deliver certitudes that will guide us. But we forget that the first certitude that he offered was the incomprehensible mystery of God that will never be completely understood despite our total effort. Jesus invites us to follow him into this mystery that always lures us to something "more" in ourselves, in others, and in our world. Whenever and however we sense ourselves being drawn beyond our present limitations, we know that God is somehow present.

According to Dutch theologian Edward Schillebeeckx, our whole existence is shaped by this divine "mystery which eludes us and is always beyond our grasp. We live in a reality which is given to us as God's gift. We live as strangers in this reality, yet we are at the same time invited to accept it, and we therefore experience it explicitly as a mystery and thus as a gift. But it is in this reality that we are permitted to live and discover our well-being" (*The Eucharist,* p. 128).

2. Jesus' Human Experience Involves Life, Death, and Resurrection

Each of us carries a mental portrait of Jesus. It is like a mosaic that has been composed of many tiny fragments of information. Our personal portrait does not exactly coincide with anyone else's but is shaped to give us the Jesus we need most.

But during that process of shaping our own picture of Jesus, we pick and choose what we want to use. We use Scripture taken out of context to back up our positions, and we often conveniently overlook or disregard what to us seems irrelevant, unhelpful, or unattractive. Of course, what we often reject first are the hard sayings, the challenging questions, and the puzzling deeds with which Jesus confronts us.

While this process of shaping our own Jesus is essential, we cannot forget that the many facets of Jesus' life—his words and deeds, his miracles and meals, his teaching and mission, his death and resurrection—are part of a bigger picture. When, through faith, we commit ourselves to be Jesus' disciples, we commit ourselves to the whole person, not just the parts we relate to most easily or that are most attractive to us.

So it is important that we discover those dimensions of Jesus that we are inclined to leave out of our portrait. For this reason, we need to go back again and again to the Gospel sources, not only questioning them but also allowing them to question us. As in any relationship, when we are no longer willing to pay close attention to the other, when we cease to be surprised by the other or dare to ask questions or be challenged by the questions that the other puts to us, then perhaps the relationship is no longer as serious as we might think. If we can make Jesus more manageable by applying a simple label or definition, it becomes much easier to dismiss him. But we are transformed more completely as we allow ourselves to know the more complete Jesus.

3. Jesus Was Genuinely Both Human and Divine, without Mixture or Confusion

This simple truth expresses one of the two essential Christian beliefs. Along with the trinitarian character of God, this truth distinguishes Christians from others who believe in God. It took the church almost four hundred years of sustained prayer and theological reflection to formulate it in this way at the Council of Chalcedon (A.D. 451). But we must recognize that this statement is only an affirmation of the truth of a divine mystery, not its explanation. We affirm *that* this is true, but no theologian or church pronouncement has ever, or will ever, fully explain *how* it can be so.

The tendency in Christolatry is to project divinity into Jesus in such a way that it makes him less than genuinely human. A common example of this would be the claim that Jesus had perfect and completely detailed knowledge of the future; he was born with a kind of videotape of his life, and he just played out the tape, going through the motions to fulfill what had been predetermined for him to do. Unfortunately, this eliminates the genuine humanity of Jesus.

No human has a detailed knowledge of the future. We can imagine what might happen to us later today or tomorrow or in any future situation. But since the future always hinges on choices that we and others make, envisioning the future cannot be spelled out in detail by any genuinely human person before it happens. If Jesus was just playing out a script that someone else had written for him, then where was his free choice? If Jesus had divine and perfect knowledge of everything, then where was his human mind that was limited and had to learn from experience?

He wakes desires you never may forget;
　　He shows you stars you never saw before;
He makes you share with Him forevermore
　　The burden of the world's divine regret.

—*ALFRED, LORD TENNYSON*
(1809–1892), British poet

We are drawn to Jesus because he was a genuine human being. Of course, his followers began to realize that he was more than just a human, but until the Resurrection, exactly what this "more" consisted of was rather vague. So even though we can affirm that Jesus was divine and human, we have no inkling of how Jesus experienced being divine. But we can still resonate with how he experienced being human. He was just like us, "yet without sin" (Heb 4:15).

How would being human without any sin manifest itself? If sin is a generic term for what breaks down relationships, then Jesus' whole life was one in which he never did anything that damaged or broke down his relationships with God or with others. In other words, he lived a human life in the most authentic, most human way possible.

FOR THE SEEKER GOING FURTHER

4. Jesus Is Our Model of an Authentic Human Person

Because Jesus lived the most exemplary human life in relation to God and others, what he did ought to become the model for us. Jesus taught us the ABCs of human existence. His attitudes, beliefs, and commitments show us what it means to be authentically human.

Just as the meaning of an event must be put in a larger context if we are to discover its significance, so the days of our lives are understood only in the larger context of the years and decades of life. But how can a person discover the meaning of his or her *whole life?* What larger picture exists that allows us to find our true significance?

Through the life of Jesus, God provided that larger picture. The whole pattern of Jesus' life—birth, youth, adulthood, public ministry, death, and resurrection—revealed the genuine pattern of all human existence in relation to God. Jesus' story is our story too. Each of us is a beloved child of God, loved into existence and made for relationships. When we realize that this is our vocation, or call, then our whole life becomes our response to that call. We are invited to spend ourselves in service to God's presence—recognizing it, celebrating it, and ordering our lives accordingly.

More than anything else, Jesus taught us what our lives could be if we respond to his invitation. The imitation of Christ has been a theme for Christian spirituality since the time of Paul (1 Cor 11:1). As we become more and more like

Christ, we become living examples of the gospel message—
the only gospel some persons may ever read.

5. Jesus Is Alive and Well and Eager for a Relationship

Perhaps the greatest hurdle for a would-be disciple is to
answer the question Is Jesus still dead, or has he risen to new
life? This is the ultimate foundation of the Christian faith.
If we affirm that the Jesus we have been investigating, who
lived, taught, suffered, and died two millennia ago, is now
alive and well, then the Christian life becomes a search for the
risen Jesus.

We seek the Risen One just as did those disciples to
whom he first appeared. We can search the empty tomb, but
it remains empty. The large and immovable rock that held
Jesus fast in the tomb of death has been removed by the
power of God. And as Matthew so interestingly symbolizes
it, when the angel rolls away the rock, he sits down on it
as a sign that this rock will stay put (Mt 28:2). Things have
changed. No one will ever again roll this stone back to hold
the dead in their tombs.

The risen Christ's presence, his effective influence on us,
continues through the mysterious power of God's own ener-
gizing Spirit of love. Though absent from us in body, Jesus
has sent this Spirit to continue his work on earth. Jesus
associated the gift of this Spirit with the forgiveness of sins
(Jn 20:22–23) because the Holy Spirit, the energy of divine

love, bonds all creation into right relationships. Through this Spirit, the breath of life is breathed into us and we are bonded in faith as members of the kingdom community. Through this Spirit, our minds and hearts are bonded to Jesus and thus to God in a relationship so strong that the power of death cannot break it.

Most of us will never directly experience any vision of Jesus in our lifetime. But as the Scriptures make clear, except for a privileged group of early disciples and a handful of mystics since, visions of the risen Christ need not be the starting point of the Christian relationship. The root of our faith is the Good News that what happened to Jesus will happen to us if we relate to God as he did.

Jesus' words to the doubting Thomas are still as true today as they were when John penned them: "Have you believed because you have seen me? Blessed are those who have not seen and yet have come to believe" (Jn 20:29). Even without seeing with our eyes or touching with our hands, when we can affirm with Thomas that Jesus is "my Lord and my God" (Jn 20:28), the adventure of a relationship begins.

Jesus and the Seeker's Journey

For those, then, who decide to enter a relationship with Jesus, a new journey begins that leads the seeker deeper into companionship and conversion. The final seeker's journey, then, will be a lifelong search for the risen Christ.

This journey of a lifetime has been depicted for us by the Gospel writer Luke. His famous story of the two disciples journeying to Emmaus on that first Easter morning summarizes what our Christian discipleship will be like (Lk 24:13–35).

With their hopes crushed by the tragedy of Jesus' crucifixion and utterly confused by the reports of the empty tomb and the angelic announcements that Jesus was alive, the two disciples decided to pack it in and go home. Every hope Jesus had raised as a "prophet mighty in deed and word" had gone awry. There was no future in being a disciple of Jesus.

As they trudged along, tossing the conversation back and forth, the two disciples were joined by a mysterious stranger who knew nothing at all about what had happened during the previous few days in Jerusalem.

As they walked farther with the stranger, they explained their version of what had happened. Then the stranger began to explain the Scriptures to them, opening up angles of interpretation they had never thought of. He offered a new framework in which they could understand the life and death of Jesus and so perceive more accurately its meaning.

As they drew near their destination that evening, the two disciples invited the stranger to dine with them. When he took the bread, blessed and broke it, then gave it to them, they suddenly recognized that the stranger was Jesus. In their excitement they rushed back to Jerusalem to share their good news.

In this story, we have a model for the behavior of disciples who, like us, walk on their journey between the Resurrection and the time of final fulfillment. We walk, sometimes despondent and confused, without the benefit of a vision. But our journey is blessed through the mysterious presence of Christ in our companions, in our Scriptures, and in our food for the journey.

We have companions on the journey who share our situation and perhaps our misguided faith and understanding. How often have we decided in advance what hoops God must jump through before we will believe? How often have we decided that there is not enough payoff in being a disciple? How often have we decided to give up and seek an easier way or an easier teacher?

But Jesus continues to walk with us as a mysterious stranger. One important lesson from the various accounts of the Easter appearances of Jesus is that he decides under what guise he is to appear. Whether as this stranger to the travelers, as a gardener to Mary Magdalene (Jn 20:11–18), or as a friendly guy on the shore who tells the disciples where to fish (Jn 21:4–9), Jesus assures us of his continued presence.

Matthew makes this point in another way by reporting Jesus' image of the final judgment (Mt 25:31–46). Jesus told his audience that the criteria for receiving God's reward would hinge on how we treated the poor, the hungry, the thirsty, the naked, the stranger, and those in prison. By treating them according to the guidelines for right relationships (justice grounded in love and compassion), we will be rewarded. The reward comes not merely because we have acted justly but because Jesus has hidden himself in these people we have helped. The risen Christ is revealed not only in his own body but also in the bodies of others.

If anyone had told me that Christ is outside truth, and if it had really been established that truth is outside Christ, I should have preferred to stay with Christ rather than with truth.

—*FYODOR MIKHAILOVICH DOSTOYEVSKY*
(1821–1881), Russian novelist

Just as God chose to be present in the broken body of Jesus on the cross rather than in the Jerusalem temple, so Jesus now chooses sides with the poor and the oppressed and invites us to discover him there. When we look for Jesus today, we cannot limit his presence to where we think he ought to be, for Jesus always chooses where he will appear and who will find him on the journey.

Jesus also blessed us with a map for the journey. The map for our journey is found in our Scriptures. Just as Jesus was God's Word made flesh, so the Scriptures are God's Word made text. What God thinks and imagines becomes known to us through the expression of the divine words. These

FOR THE SEEKER GOING FURTHER

words are our primary source for understanding the hidden mystery of God's personal being and for learning what God's activity is in relation to us.

The Scriptures tell the story of God's revelation to us in the people of Israel (the Old Testament or covenant relationship) and in Jesus (the New Testament). This revelation of God's mysterious self occurs through saving deeds and personal words that work together. "As a result, the works performed by God in the history of salvation show forth and bear out the doctrine and realities signified by the words; the words, for their part, proclaim the works, and bring to light the mystery they contain. The most intimate truth which this revelation gives us about God and human salvation shines forth in Christ, who is himself both the mediator and the sum total of Revelation" (Vatican Council II, *Dogmatic Constitution on Divine Revelation [Dei Verbum]*, #2, modified Flannery translation).

On the way to Emmaus, Jesus opened up a new meaning of the Scriptures to his companions. They had read the same words of the text as Jesus had, but they had missed the meaning he saw. How often have we read the words but missed the meaning because our viewpoint was too narrow, our categories too rigid, and our minds too closed?

Jesus reminds us that we go to the Scriptures as his disciples and must read them through the lens of his death and resurrection. This is the interpretive key to understanding who God is and how badly God wants to be in a relationship with us. It also offers us insight into how we ought to respond to God.

Jesus has also blessed us with food for the journey. The companions on the road and in the conversation about the meaning of Scripture become true companions at the meal. The word *companion* identifies those whom we share bread with (Latin, *cum,* "with" and *panis,* "bread") and so metaphorically those with whom we share life.

But the bread that Jesus provides is himself, body and blood. The Emmaus disciples recognize the identity of the mysterious stranger only in the companionship meal. When the stranger performs the same actions that constitute our Eucharist—take, bless, break, share—they know it is Jesus.

But the mystery of this eucharistic bread is that when we eat and digest it, instead of eating and digesting this food so that it becomes part of our body and a source of energy for living, we are transformed into the body of Christ and participate in an energy that gives us life everlasting.

Through this sacred ritual, we are drawn into that larger and more mysterious reality that was mentioned earlier. Through our participation in this companionship meal with the risen Lord each Sunday, we become what we eat: the body of Jesus Christ. The promised transformation anticipated by our resurrection begins now.

FOR THE SEEKER GOING FURTHER

Through our relationship with Jesus, we recognize that his words to us from long ago still offer an answer to our deepest yearnings. But our search for the risen Christ ends up being curiously reversed. Our search for Jesus has really been God's search for us. Instead of finding him, he has secretly found us. We, the seekers, have always been the sought.

Master, to whom shall we go?

—*JOHN 6:68*

CHAPTER FOURTEEN

Reading the Gospels

As the Chinese proverb reminds us, "Teachers open the door, but you must enter by yourself." For the reader who wants to continue his or her search for Jesus in the Gospels, I am recommending further resources that have been most helpful to me. My criteria are that they be user friendly, blending solid and accurate scholarship with readability.

Reading the Gospels

Your first task after finishing this *Seeker's Guide to Jesus in the Gospels* ought to be a careful reading of the four Gospel accounts of the life, death, and resurrection of Jesus. Despite various arguments to the contrary, these Gospels are still the most reliable reports about who Jesus was and what he did.

Unlike readers today, who presume that these documents are "objective" news reports relating somehow only the "facts" about Jesus, the ancient audience took for granted that these Gospels, like all speech and communication, had a persuasive agenda. They represent the Christian community's memory and message—the Good News—about the facts and the significance of Jesus' life, death, and resurrection.

A good way to begin is to read each Gospel straight through, as though it were a modern short story or novel. Don't get bogged down in the details but appreciate the drama and sweep of the whole story. It is very important to read the Gospels in a modern translation, preferably one like the New American Bible (NAB), the New Revised Standard Version (NRSV), or the New International Version (NIV). For more detailed comments on biblical translations and various helps for biblical study, see my *Seeker's Guide to Reading the Bible: A Catholic View* (Loyola, 1999).

If you need to purchase a new Bible, you might consider a study Bible as a way of acquiring both a modern translation and some convenient study helps. Most study Bibles include maps, extensive notes and application helps, historical and literary background, and a glossary or brief dictionary of important terms.

A very good investment for the serious seeker would be one of the two excellent study Bibles published by Oxford University Press, *The Catholic Study Bible* (1990) or *The*

Catholic Bible: Personal Study Edition (1995). These include the complete New American Bible together with background articles and extremely helpful reading guides for every book of the Bible. The *HarperCollins Study Bible* includes the NRSV translation and excellent notes written by an ecumenical group of biblical scholars that included several Catholics. There are numerous study Bibles that use the NIV translation.

Consulting a Bible Dictionary or Encyclopedia

For quick information about the people, places, things, and themes that you encounter in your reading, consult a Bible dictionary or encyclopedia. The best single-volume ones are John L. McKenzie's *Dictionary of the Bible* (Macmillan), which not only gives biblical information but also relates this to Catholic theology, *Harper's Bible Dictionary,* or the *Oxford Dictionary of the Bible.*

There are also several multivolume resources such as the five-volume *Interpreter's Dictionary of the Bible* and the six-volume *Anchor Bible Dictionary,* which is the finest and most up-to-date multivolume encyclopedia available. It also comes on a CD-ROM for your home computer (available through Logos Research Systems).

The *Anchor Bible Dictionary* article on Jesus Christ, for example, contains excellent summaries of what we know about Jesus from various source documents, his sociohistorical context, and his life, including a consideration of his beginnings, his teaching, his identity and destiny, why and how he died, and the meaning of the Easter experience of the disciples.

Using a Commentary

After you have read the four Gospels for yourself, you can work through each one more carefully with the aid of a commentary, which discusses the meanings of the biblical text. Commentaries are numerous and come in various degrees of difficulty.

Beginning commentaries take you through the text in larger units so that you get the general flavor of the biblical book. They provide enough detail to enhance your reading but not so much that you bog down. Perhaps the most helpful Catholic commentary on this level is the *Collegeville Bible Commentary.* Covering every book of the Bible, these come individually in a handy pamphlet size and include the NAB text on the top part of the page and the running commentary below. Study questions are also included. The complete commentary, without the Bible text, is also published in separate Old and New Testament volumes or in a convenient single-volume edition.

Intermediate level commentaries add more detailed information and cover the biblical text almost verse by verse. Examples of this type include the several volumes in the as yet incomplete *Sacra Pagina* series from Liturgical Press, the Interpretation commentaries for teaching and preaching from Westminster/John Knox, or the twelve-volume *New Interpreter's Bible* and the several *Abingdon New Testament Commentaries* from Abingdon Press. These commentaries are readable and yet challenging because they open up depths of meaning that the supposedly obvious biblical texts often conceal.

Future historians . . . are likely to conclude that the more we knew about Jesus the less we knew him, and the more precisely his words were translated the less we understood or heeded them.

—*MALCOLM MUGGERIDGE*
author, historian

Advanced commentaries are those that scholars use for a detailed analysis of the text. You can often read these with great profit when you wish to explore specific verses or puzzling passages in greater depth.

There are also one-volume Bible commentaries containing explanations of each biblical book. Examples include *Harper's Bible Commentary, The International Bible Commentary, The Interpreter's One-Volume Commentary on the Bible,* the *NIV Bible Companion,* and *The Women's Bible Commentary.*

The finest Catholic example of a one-volume commentary is the *New Jerome Biblical Commentary* (Prentice-Hall,

1990) edited by Fr. Raymond Brown, Fr. Joseph Fitzmyer, and Fr. Roland Murphy. Besides thorough introductions and a detailed commentary for each biblical book, this volume has more than twenty topical articles covering the basic material that any seeker would want to know about the Bible. If there were only one book to put in your home reference library, this would be it.

Jesus and His World

An atlas of biblical lands, with its historical and geographical maps, is helpful for situating Jesus in his physical environment. There are many to choose from. *The Hammond Atlas of the Bible* is inexpensive and yet contains excellent maps. Others to look at include *The Macmillan Bible Atlas, The Harper Atlas of the Bible,* and *The Oxford Bible Atlas.* Many Bible computer programs also include maps.

John J. Rousseau & Rami Arav have produced *Jesus and His World: An Archaeological and Cultural Dictionary* (Fortress, 1995), a helpful summary of archeological and historical information about the time of Christ. E. P. Sanders's *Judaism: Practice and Belief 63 BCE–66 CE* (SCM/Trinity, 1992) opens up the world of common Judaism that Jesus and his contemporaries would have been familiar with.

Bruce Malina and Richard Rohrbaugh's *Social Science Commentary on the Synoptic Gospels* (Fortress, 1992) and

Social Science Commentary on the Gospel of John (Fortress, 1998) present verse-by-verse commentary on the social and cultural background needed to understand the Gospels in their first-century milieu. John J. Pilch and Bruce Malina's *Biblical Social Values and Their Meaning* (Hendrickson, 1993) explains the cultural values, such as honor and shame, that characterized Jesus' culture and underlie the Gospel writers' presentation of his life and ministry.

Working with a Synopsis of the Gospels

As you continue to study the Gospels more thoroughly, you might wish to purchase a synopsis, which places the texts side by side in order to detect more easily the changes among the particular Gospels. This allows you to study the unique contributions of each evangelist just as the scholars do in what they call *redaction* (editing) *criticism.* Burton Throckmorton's *Gospel Parallels* (Thomas Nelson and Sons) is a synopsis of the first three Gospels. Its older editions (1949–92) used the Revised Standard Version (RSV), and a newly revised edition (1993) uses the NRSV text. *A Synopsis of the Four Gospels,* edited by Kurt Aland, is available from the American Bible Society.

READING THE GOSPELS

Books on the Historical Jesus

The last decade of the twentieth century witnessed a flurry of scholarly publication concerning the historical Jesus. The scholarly debates often spilled over into media coverage that made Jesus a hot topic. Instead of trying to cover all these materials, I will mention only a few of the more important contributions that I have found most helpful.

To survey the whole development of modern scholarship about Jesus, one could read chapters 1–3 of N. T. Wright's *Jesus and the Victory of God* (Fortress, 1996) or the longer treatment by Ben Witherington III, *The Jesus Quest: The Third Search for the Jew of Nazareth* (InterVarsity Press, 1995).

The Understanding Jesus Today series from Cambridge University Press offers excellent short books that acquaint readers with basic issues and concerns. They are written by an international group of highly respected Scripture scholars representing several Christian denominations.

What Can We Know About Jesus by Howard Clark Kee (1990).

The World of Jesus by John K. Riches (1990).

Jesus and the Future by David L. Tiede (1990).

Jesus as Teacher by Pheme Perkins (1990).

Jesus' Call to Discipleship by James D. G. Dunn (1992).

Jesus According to Paul by Victor Paul Furnish (1993).

Jesus as Healer by Harold Remus (1997).

FOR THE SEEKER GOING FURTHER

Several of the scholars who have been influential in revitalizing and reconfiguring Jesus research have written more popular and readable books that summarize the conclusions of their scholarly publications. Of the popular books, I recommended that by E. P. Sanders, which is not only very readable but clearly summarizes the data. The most helpful scholarly book is that by N. T. Wright, who masterfully draws together the overwhelming mass of data and offers thought provoking and insightful connections and explanations. He also includes an extensive and helpful bibliography.

E. P. Sanders

(popular) *The Historical Figure of Jesus* (Penguin, 1993).
(scholarly) *Jesus and Judaism* (Fortress, 1985).

N. T. Wright

(popular) *The Original Jesus: The Life and Vision of a Revolutionary* (Eerdmans, 1996).
The Challenge of Jesus: Rediscovering Who Jesus Was and Is (InterVarsity Press, 1999).
(scholarly) *Jesus and the Victory of God* (Fortress, 1997).

Other important contributions include:

Marcus Borg

(popular) *Jesus, a New Vision: Spirit, Culture, and the Life of Discipleship* (HarperSanFrancisco, 1987).

*Meeting Jesus Again for the First Time: The Historical Jesus
and the Heart of Contemporary Faith*
(HarperSanFrancisco, 1994).

(scholarly) *Conflict, Holiness, and Politics in the Teachings of
Jesus* (Trinity Press International, 1998).

John Dominic Crossan

(popular) *Jesus: A Revolutionary Biography*
(HarperSanFrancisco, 1994).

(scholarly) *The Historical Jesus: The Life of a Mediterranean
Jewish Peasant* (HarperSanFrancisco, 1991).

Luke Timothy Johnson

*The Real Jesus: The Misguided Quest for the Historical Jesus
and the Truth of the Traditional Gospels*
(HarperSanFrancisco, 1997).

Living Jesus: Learning the Heart of the Gospel
(HarperSanFrancisco, 1999).

John P. Meier

(scholarly) *A Marginal Jew: Rethinking the Historical Jesus*
(Doubleday, two volumes).

Vol. 1. *The Roots of the Problem and the Person* (1991).

Vol. 2. *Mentor, Message, and Miracles* (1994).

Gerd Theissen

(popular) *The Shadow of the Galilean: The Quest of the
Historical Jesus in Narrative Form* (Fortress, 1987).

(scholarly) With Annette Merz, *The Historical Jesus: A Comprehensive Guide* (Fortress, 1998).

To become acquainted with the issues and debates among these scholars, one could consult:

Mark Alan Powell. *Jesus as a Figure in History: How Modern Historians View the Man from Galilee* (Westminster John Knox, 1998). **John Dominic Crossan, Luke Timothy Johnson, Werner H. Kelber,** *The Jesus Controversy: Perspectives in Conflict* (Trinity Press International, 1999). **Marcus J. Borg and N. T. Wright**, *The Meaning of Jesus: Two Visions* (HarperSanFrancisco, 1999).

Other Issues Related to Jesus

Raymond E. Brown, *The Death of the Messiah: From Gethsemane to the Grave. A Commentary on the Passion Narratives in the Four Gospels* (Doubleday, 1994).

Eugene LaVerdiere, *Dining in the Kingdom of God: The Origins of the Eucharist According to Luke* (Liturgy Training Publications, 1994).

Bernard Brandon Scott, *Hear Then the Parable: A Commentary on the Parables of Jesus* (Fortress, 1989).

Donald Senior, The Passion of Jesus series [four volumes, one on each Gospel] (Liturgical Press, 1984–91).

Finally, if you wish to investigate how the Christian understanding of Jesus found in the Gospels developed into the doctrinal formulations of the church, you might want to explore:

(popular) Jaroslav Pelikan's wonderful presentation of *Jesus through the Centuries: His Place in the History of Culture* (Yale University Press, 1985), also available in a beautifully illustrated version (1997).

(scholarly) Gerald O'Collins, *Christology: A Biblical, Historical, and Systematic Study of Jesus* (Oxford University Press, 1995).

Enjoy Your Search!

These, then, are some recommendations that will help you continue your Jesus quest. Using any of these resources will lead you to other books and authors that will guide you further. As with any search, one thing always leads to another, one path opens upon another, one interest yields to a new one, and one question answered spawns more questions.

Yet I am confident that you will discover the Jesus you search for. The advice that Jesus gave seekers long ago still applies.

Ask, and it will be given you;
search, and you will find;

knock, and the door will be opened for you.
For everyone who asks receives,
and everyone who searches finds,
and for everyone who knocks,
the door will be opened.

—MATTHEW 7:7–8

A Reader's Guide

Since many readers enjoy sharing their seeker's journey to discover Jesus in the Gospels, this seeker's guide provides questions to stimulate personal reflection and group discussion. Use of these questions can be adapted to suit a variety of needs, time frames, purposes, and formats.

The questions in this reader's guide can be used

- by individual seekers or by groups interested in faith sharing or Bible study
- to discuss the book chapter by chapter, in sections, or as a whole, depending on whether you are holding brief weekly sessions or are meeting less frequently but for a longer period of time
- to generate additional questions, according to the interests and goals of your group
- by seekers of all ages and interests—adults in study or faith-sharing groups, those investigating the Christian faith for the first time, or teens in high school or college

inquiring on a more mature level about their beliefs concerning Jesus.

Chapter 1: Seeking the Identity of Jesus

As you begin your search for the identity of Jesus, which will in turn change and shape your own identity, spend some time reflecting, writing, and discussing with fellow seekers your answers to the following questions.

- What are you looking for?
- Why do you want to learn about Jesus?
- What do you want to learn from him?
- How can Jesus the teacher help you with your search?
- Where has most of your information and knowledge about Jesus come from?
- What is it about Jesus that fascinates and puzzles you most?

Chapter 2: Jesus, the Nazarene

- How did Jesus' experience as a male influence his outlook and ministry?
- When have stereotypes helped you cope with a strange situation?

- When have stereotypes not been helpful in getting to know another person?
- How might Jesus' experience in the border area of Galilee have influenced his outlook on strangers?

Chapter 3: Jesus, the Son of Mary and Joseph

- Why is the designation of Jesus as "son" a helpful key to understanding his identity?
- What are the similarities and differences between your household and a first-century one?
- Why might Jesus choose to identify his disciples as a kind of family?
- How might an understanding of Jesus as a more mature man change your media stereotype of him?

Chapter 4: Jesus, the Jewish Messiah

- How might a deeper appreciation of Jesus' Jewishness influence your understanding of and behavior toward Jews?
- What kind of liberation are you most in need of?
- What kind of liberator can bring about this liberation for you?

- Why wouldn't Jesus accept any of the preconceived Jewish ideas of messiah to describe his role?
- How would you describe the ideal messiah for people today?
- Can Jesus fulfill this job description? Why, or why not?

Chapter 5: Jesus, the Bearer of the New Age

- How does the book of Daniel tie into Jesus' self-description of "Son of man"?
- Why would "Son of man" mean more than Jesus simply being human?
- Describe the different meanings of "Son of man" and how they related to Jesus.

Chapter 6: Jesus, the Son of God

- What are the different types of sonship?
- How did each of the four Gospel writers explain Jesus' divine sonship?
- Why is the role of a messenger so appropriate for John's understanding of Jesus?
- How can each Christian fulfill the obligations of the messenger role today?

Chapter 7: Jesus' Goal: Building God's Kingdom

- How would you summarize Jesus' overall goal or aim for his ministry?
- In what ways do you make this goal your own?
- Why would Jesus think of God as a patron?
- In what ways have you experienced God providing for you and protecting you?
- How does our prayer reflect the working of a client-patron relationship?

Chapter 8: Jesus the Prophet: Disclosing God's Presence

- Why would people identify Jesus as one of the prophets?
- What was Jesus' prophetic task?
- Was his strategy of using parables effective? Why or why not?
- In what ways does a Christian continue the prophetic work of Jesus?
- Describe a situation when you acted prophetically, calling attention to God's hidden presence in a particular situation.

Chapter 9: Jesus the Priest: Celebrating God's Presence

- Why was Jesus considered a priest although he was not a minister in the temple or from a priestly family?

- What was Jesus' priestly task?

- How did Jesus carry out this task? Why was or why wasn't this effective?

- In what ways does a Christian continue the priestly work of Jesus?

- Describe a situation when you acted in a priestly way, mediating communion with God or celebrating God's presence with others in a ritualized way.

Chapter 10: Jesus the King: Reordering Life in God's Presence

- What was Jesus' kingly task?

- Was his choice of a strategy to accomplish it effective? Why or why not?

- Can miracles still happen? Why or why not?

- In what ways does a Christian continue the kingly work of Jesus?

- How does each Christian perform "deeds of power" that reorder life as God wishes it to be?

- Describe a situation when you acted in a kingly way, reordering life according to God's presence or with God's priorities.

Chapter 11: Jesus Who Suffered and Died

- How would you explain the conflict between Jesus and the Jewish leaders?
- What is the importance of the temple controversy in this conflict?
- How does Jesus' death connect to his kingdom ministry?
- What does it mean to say that Mark invented the written Passion narrative for his Gospel?
- Indicate two or three ways that Jesus is portrayed as God's honorable Son during his trial and crucifixion.

Chapter 12: Jesus Who Rose from the Dead

- What is the difference between resuscitation and resurrection?
- What is the connection of the Resurrection to God's power?
- What is the connection of the Resurrection to God's love?
- Explain to a friend why Christians thought that the Resurrection was "according to the scriptures."

A READER'S GUIDE

- Why would Christians consider the resurrection of Jesus a reward for his honorable behavior?
- What makes the Resurrection "news"? What makes this news "good"?

Chapter 13: Following Christ Today

- Think back on your life and note significant experiences of God's presence to you. How were you changed by this experience?
- What can you recall about your "call" or invitation to follow Jesus in a more adult way? What attracted you or made you turn to Jesus?
- How has your "faith commitment" to Jesus changed over the years? What has helped make it stronger or weaker?
- In what ways is God prodding you to new levels of relationship to Jesus?
- In what ways is God inviting you to new levels of holiness by prayer?
- What resistance do you experience that keeps you from following these promptings?
- In what ways is God bringing you to a new awareness of God's values?